GENERATIONS OF FAITH

CARL G. EEMAN

FOREWORD BY WILLIAM STRAUSS AND NEIL HOWE

AN ALBAN INSTITUTE PUBLICATION

Copyright © 2002 by the Alban Institute. All rights reserved.

This material may not be photocopied or reproduced in any way without written permission.

Library of Congress Card Number 2002109033

ISBN I-56699-272-9

To Vera, Gunnar, Wanda, and Clarence, and all the generations

before who walked in the paths of the Lord.

To Heather, who walks beside me as we follow his call.

To Vivi, Jim, Chris, and Staci, and all of these

generations who live in these days.

To Annelise, Marcus, Julia, Laurel, Mark, Emma,

and all of their generations yet to come, who will see

treasures of the Lord, both old and new.

Contents

In the early 1990s, soon after we published our first book on generations, we were surprised to encounter an unusual amount of interest in this subject by national church groups. By mail or by phone, they sought us out. They wanted us to tell them more about some of the seismic attitude and behavior changes they saw transforming their members in all of their various age strata. They noticed "senior citizens" holding on to institutional power in ways that seemed new to them. They saw 60-somethings yearning for more discussion, more process, yet also more experimentation. They saw argumentative 40-somethings lurch back and forth between detachment and commitment (a Boomer habit sometimes wryly referred to as "elective orthodoxy"). And they saw 20-somethings tune out, drift off, or simply never show up.

"What's happening?" these leaders asked. "Are we changing, are they changing, are the times changing?" "None of those things," We would tell them. "What's happening is that you were all different to begin with. You were shaped differently by history. You belong to different generations." After a moment's reflection, few of these leaders had any trouble grasping this answer. In fact, once they caught on, we often found they had much to teach us on the subject.

The question we soon wanted to ask them was why church personnel seemed so unusually sensitive to generational change and so quick to understand its consequences. The answer, we learned, was that you can appreciate generational change precisely to the extent that your work requires you to take a broad view of the people around you. Those who work in churches typically do take a very broad view. They work with people in all walks of life and in all of their life roles—as parents and as children, as spouses and as siblings, as bosses and as workers, as winners and as losers. They work with people in every emotional and spiritual condition, from blessed to cursed. And, of course, they work with people of all ages. They need to understand the memories of the old as well as the dreams of the young.

Lots of professionals would like to master the dynamics of generational change. There's the veteran HR manager asked to design a new retirement plan for the executives in his firm. Or there's the rookie marketer of a new lipstick brand who really needs a homerun response from the young and hip "Buffy" crowd. But try as they might, many of them will never get it. Church people, on the other hand, nearly always get it—once it's explained clearly and completely to them.

That brings us to Carl Eeman's excellent new book. There are, to be honest, a fair number of monographs now in print that examine changing religious attitudes from a generational perspective. Some of them stress survey data. Others focus on one particular age group. Still others have prompted entire new discussion sites on the Web. (Much of this new interest in a generational approach to changing currents in religion has grown up over the last decade, which is gratifying to those of us who have been encouraging it.)

But anyone looking for a comprehensive overview of how and why generational aging transforms religion over time cannot turn to a better resource than this one. Yes, Carl borrows our generations and "turnings" model—but this frankly does not bias our judgment. The first purpose of any model is simply to compel readers to think. And we wouldn't care which model is chosen so long as it explores the full depth and significance of generational differences (that is, how they are associated with essentially distinct worldviews or temperaments) and so long as it takes the long view and explores such differences over history. Carl's book accomplishes both objectives. It is therefore a success.

Having known Carl for several years, we can attest to his dedication to widening our understanding of this vast subject. He speaks to church groups often and eloquently. He has an eye for the luminous detail. And he never takes his mind off the big picture.

We are especially impressed by Carl's interpretation of the quaternity of generational personality types, a four-fold typology that is as ancient as the classical temperaments and as contemporary as the Myers-Briggs Type Indicator. From Homer to Hesiod, the pagan myths of antiquity often applied such mandala-like patterns to the succession of "races" or "generations" of men—as does the inspired biblical Book of Daniel, which outlines a sequential rhythm of generational archetypes that appears more than once in the Old Testament. Reflect, for example, on the generation of Moses, followed by the generation of the golden calf, then of Joshua, and then of the first judges. Or the generation of Samuel, then of Saul, then of David, and then of Solomon. Carl alludes to such examples while explaining how these patterns work, and he supplements them with a theological quaternity, adapted from the Christian trinity, which we find both thought provoking and entirely original.

Most of all, he shows how these generational ebbs and flows have shaped the spiritual lives of the Americans over the last half century, an era in which we have seen so much change in how our society thinks about religion—from an emphasis on works, then on faith, and now (perhaps) back toward works again.

What will happen to today's rising generation, and where will they find God? Will the spiritual virtues of their grandparents die forever, or will they reappear? When can parents take pride in practicing the creed or liturgy of their own parents, and when should they worry about repeating their parents' mistakes with their own kids? In the midst of all this generational flux, how can church leaders be most helpful?

If you've ever puzzled over such questions, you have picked up the right book. Absorb the panorama, and enjoy the read.

NEIL HOWE (WITH WILLIAM STRAUSS)
Coauthors of
Generations and *The Fourth Turning:
An American Prophecy*

In 1991 a pair of Ivy League–educated Californians, William Strauss and Neil Howe, published a landmark book, *Generations: The History of America's Future from 1584 to 2069*. In *Generations* and subsequent books they develop a theory of *generational types* cycling through American history at about 90- to 95-year intervals. Their contribution rests on a combination of sociological insights and careful observations of American history. From sociology they bring the concepts of age cohorts and peer personalities, and the ideas that a given generation holds common beliefs, exhibits similar behaviors, and perceives itself as a generation. From American history they add the factors of sustained immigration, the lack of a European-style caste system, and the open frontier (beginning with the forests of Massachusetts Bay all the way to the Pacific). In combination these factors have allowed a generational rhythm to emerge.

Four distinct types follow each other in a set order through four stages of life. Each type, especially as it moves through the leadership stage of life (approximately ages 45-65) makes unique generational contributions to society and its institutions, including religious bodies. For instance, one type builds and expands physical infrastructure, another refines and civilizes social conventions, a third re-examines and reforms social institutions, and a fourth takes high risks and tests out new ideas and processes.

Strauss and Howe note that generations, like individuals, pass through four stages of life. They draw divisions at 22-year intervals for youth (birth through age 21), rising adulthood (22–44), midlife (45–66), and elderhood (66-plus). Each stage of life has a prime focus.

Stage of Life	Prime Focus
Youth	Dependence
Rising Adulthood	Activity
Midlife	Leadership
Elderhood	Stewardship

In this book I accept Strauss and Howe's invitation, as issued in *Generations*: "We encourage specialists among our readers, whatever their backgrounds, to shed more light on the component pieces of the generational puzzle."[1] This book explores the cycle of four generational types from a faith perspective, applying generational insights to the practice of ministry and congregational issues.

As Strauss and Howe are still defining the field of generational ideas, they employ several terms in their books for the four generational types. *Idealist* or *Prophet* describes one type of generation. (The Boomers are the current generation of this type.) I use Idealist, because Prophet may carry confusing connotations. For a second type, Strauss and Howe alternate between *Adaptive* and *Artist*. I use Adaptive, since I think each generational type makes an artistic mark. A third type Strauss and Howe term *Civic* and *Hero*; I use Civic because every generation produces its own heroes. Finally, Strauss and Howe describe the fourth type of generation as *Reactive* and *Nomad*. Here I use Nomad—reactive seems to convey a certain passivity, while the wayfaring character of a nomad has often suited such generations. Within each type are more familiar generational labels like Baby Boomers or Generation Xers, but these are current manifestations of the repeating types.

In my opinion, each generational type has its own perspective on "the faith once delivered to the saints" [Jude 3, RSV], emphasizing certain perspectives, doctrines, and aspects of God while downplaying or ignoring other aspects. By offering its own perspective, each generational type refreshes the ongoing theological conversation among the people of God.

Strauss and Howe offer a compelling pair of statements about the relationship between history and generations: History shapes generations. Generations shape history. Chapters 1 and 2 look at how the circumstances and expectations of history are conveyed from adults to children (and later, more directly to young adults)—filtered, explained, amplified, or blocked. (For example, Idealist parents tend to raise children, and hence a generation, to be team players. Civic parents raise children to be free thinkers.) Parents, schools, and religion have a major (though steadily decreasing) influence in a generation's early years. In adolescence and early adulthood these early influences are replaced by peer pressure, economic opportunities and expectations, generational self-understanding, family-formation patterns, and religious and spiritual assumptions. All these factors form, shape, and color the values, attitudes, and expectations of children, adolescents, and young adults, producing one of four generational personalities.

As a rule, a generation produces and rears children who are *two* generational types behind them in life. If a generational cycle is composed of four generational types, following in the same order through one cycle, and each generation includes about 22 years of births, then parents and children line up like this:

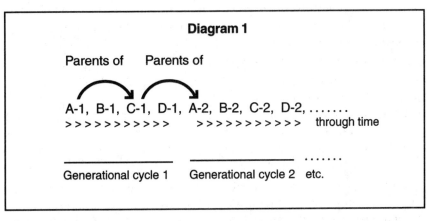

Diagram 1

Parents of   Parents of

A-1, B-1, C-1, D-1, A-2, B-2, C-2, D-2, ...
> > > > > > > > > > >   > > > > > > > > > > >   through time

Generational cycle 1   Generational cycle 2   etc.

Members of generation type A in cycle 1 give birth to and raise children of type C in cycle 1. When these children grow up and raise families of their own, they tend to raise children of type A in cycle 2.

A second factor affecting parenting of generations in youth is that at any given time, two of the generations are engaged in raising families. The *older* of the two parenting generations sets the pace for child-rearing, imposing its outlook and values.

The assumptions and values acquired early in life by members of a generation persist as a generational type for the life of the members. People of other generations expect members of a given generation to reflect the type's generational traits. Similarly, members of that generation sense these expected traits and tend to conform to them. Individuals who do not conform gain attention, even notoriety.

Strauss and Howe's second proposition—that generations shape history—becomes prominent as generations move into the latter two stages of life, traced in chapters 3 and 4. Particularly at midlife (chapter 3), when the life-cycle task is leadership, generations are providing answers to history's questions. Since institutional and cultural leaders live out their generation's values in their own settings, what is considered socially beneficial or harmful changes from generation to generation. This prominence of each generation's values has both benefits and costs for social institutions. Adaptives value freedom and self-expression, but at the cost of responsibility and discipline. Nomads value survival and security, but often stifle emotional expression and become wary of grand causes. Civics value cooperation and community, but in their eras individuality and creativity suffer. Idealists value individuality and spiritual experiences, but they often neglect the common good and the comfort of tradition.

Religious leaders highlight certain doctrines of the faith and redraw constitutions to embody changes in congregational power dynamics. Each generational type's leaders change the prevailing view of the immanence or transcendence of God, and shift the understanding of the desirable balance between justice and mercy. They build up or depreciate denominational distinctiveness and loyalty, and revisit formerly settled ecumenical arrangements.

Finally in elderhood (chapter 4) each of the four generational types shows distinctive reactions to physical decline, to the approach of death, and to the legacy it will leave to future generations. Each generational type is treated differently in elderhood by the rest of society, all of whom are now younger. Idealist generations are often honored and followed (and sometimes feared) in their old age, while members of Nomad generations are frequently neglected and ignored. Younger generations look to the Adaptive type in elderhood for emotional support and understanding, while senior members of Civic generations are often seen primarily as a source of family funding.

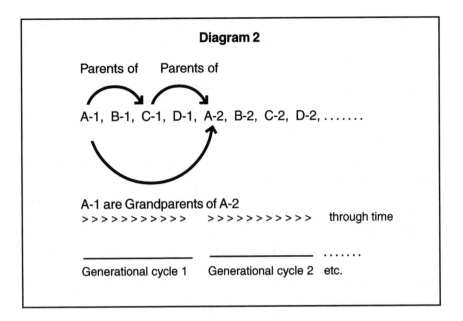

Diagram 2

Parents of   Parents of

A-1, B-1, C-1, D-1, A-2, B-2, C-2, D-2, ...

A-1 are Grandparents of A-2
> > > > > > > > > >   > > > > > > > > > > >   through time

Generational cycle 1   Generational cycle 2   etc.

As the generations move in a cycle, a generational type reappears in youth at a time when the same type is late in elderhood. The grandchildren of generation A in cycle 1 are the A generation of cycle 2. The upshot is the much-noted bond between grandparents and their grandchildren. Both of them were or are being raised by parents applying a similar set of values and assumptions.

Chapters 5 through 8 contain what might be called generational biographies. These chapters trace each generational type's life cycle through the eyes and events of 20th century generations and their historical parallels from earlier cycles. These chapters also explore religious leadership characteristics among clergy and laity—the faith assumptions and communication strengths and liabilities for each type.

The factors forming and affecting each type, and each type's particular influence are traced (using types and labels developed or used by Strauss and Howe). Included are the Adaptive Silent generation, born 1925–1942 (chapter 5); the Idealist Boom generation, born 1943–1960 (chapter 6); and the Nomadic Generation X, born 1961–1982 (chapter 7). Members of the two Civic generations now living are either old or quite young—the GI generation, born 1901–1924, and the Millennial generation, born 1983 to present (chapter 8). These chapters include general information on each generational type for those unfamiliar with Strauss and Howe's work.

Finally, with four stages of life and four generational types appearing in a repeating sequence, four alignments of generational types are possible. Strauss and Howe call each of these alignments a "Turning." In particular, as members of each generational type fill the midlife stage and exercise leadership, their traits and proclivities about God and faith assume dominance. Drawing on historical and contemporary data, chapters 9 through 12 describe the clash and mesh of intergenerational values, perceptions, and understandings.

Chapter 9 examines parish life as a Civic generation comes to leadership, with its achievements and shortcomings. Chapter 10 does the same for an era of Adaptive church leadership, such as the 1980s and 1990s. Chapter 11 looks at issues in parish life as the Idealist Boom generation takes charge. In addition, this chapter looks at some of the transitional issues between the current Silent generation of leaders and the arriving Boom generation relating to power shifts, worship considerations, denominational structures, and so forth. Chapter 12 draws on historic parallels from prior cycles to describe the coming challenges and changes that will arrive as a Nomadic generation, Gen X, comes to leadership.

Generational theory is a young field. New discoveries and problematic contradictions are bound to be uncovered as more work is done. I hope this book will become a valuable tool for understanding among generations. As leaders carry out their ministry among the people of God, I hope that generational concepts will help them to be more effective leaders, clearer communicators, and more nimble troubleshooters and problem-solvers.

ACKNOWLEDGMENTS

This book would not have been possible without the help and resources of many people and organizations. I would like to thank managing editor David Lott of the Alban Institute for his encouragement of the idea, and his able assistant Simon Hyoun for tending to the details that make a difference.

I owe a great debt to my editor, Beth Ann Gaede. Her endless patience with this first-time writer was amazing. Her persistence in pressing for clarity, conciseness, revisions, and explanations has made this a far better book than it would otherwise be. Copy editor Jean Caffey Lyles read over the final manuscript with a fine eye and a wonderful ear for language to give the writing its final polish. Thank you both so much for all your hard work.

Beth Kittelson was an early advocate of channeling my passion for the subject into book form. Neil Howe generated enthusiasm and raised thought-provoking issues in the early stages of the writing. William Strauss provided confidence and encouragement at a critical point toward the end of the project. The theological library at Luther Seminary in St. Paul, Minnesota, was an invaluable resource in supplying books, references, journals, and quiet spaces for thinking and writing.

Most deeply, my wife, Heather, and children, Annelise and Marcus, have endured a long-distracted husband and father who spent endless nights and parts of weekends clattering away at a keyboard. Their understanding, support, and cheers are beyond telling, as is their patience with me carrying on about "Nomads who believe this" or "Second Turnings that we've seen before." Thank you my loves, with all my heart.

STAGES OF LIFE

The first four chapters of this book will look at factors that shape a generation and its members in four life stages, each about 22 years long. Readers will recognize some of the attitudes and assumptions that were present as they passed through a given life stage; they may also recognize some that are present in the current stage.

As a generation matures through youth and into adulthood, it begins to modify or even resist some of the forces at work. As Strauss and Howe say, "History shapes generations," but every generation reacts differently to history. As a generation moves into the second half of life, it now does the shaping of history, particularly in its actions toward younger generations. These four chapters trace the factors that mark and shape generations, as well as the marks generations make on one another.

CHAPTER 1

A GENERATION IS BORN AND MADE

The way parents and other adults in American society view children has changed throughout our history. Attitudes, assumptions, and outlooks vary dramatically. These shifting seasons affect each generation's self-understanding, religious assumptions, and worldview.

Parenting

"How shall we raise the children?" As couples facing parenthood begin to ask this question, many factors bear on their answers. Relatives, friends, and other adults weigh in with their assumptions. Should children be kept behind certain lines with their own kind? (By gender? By race? By denomination?) Or should they be encouraged to cross such lines and revel in diversity? Other issues include family size and family structure (multigenerational? nuclear? blended? foster?) Are children wanted, or not wanted? Is the popular view of children as expressed in books, films, television, and public policies positive or negative?

In some periods society supports and reinforces parents. Idealist children typically receive increasing amounts of personal freedom to explore their inner selves. In a different period social movements encourage adults, including parents, to explore their own emotional and spiritual selves. Nomad children in these periods have often felt a lack of focus from parents and other adults and have found their own world challenging. A third period sees parents rebuilding boundaries around their children's lives. Civic children in these times find peer cooperation and outer-world achievements rewarded. In a fourth period all of society faces great external challenges. Adaptive children in these times are heavily protected and have typically been encouraged to develop emotionally rich human relationships.

To illustrate the difference between, say, the first two periods, consider 1958 and 1977. In 1958 social attitudes toward children put a high value on protection, education, and stable families. A four-in-one vaccine to protect against polio, whooping cough, diphtheria, and tetanus was successfully tested on 300 Detroit preschoolers.[1] New brick schools with aluminum-framed windows blossomed across the suburbs and into rural consolidated districts. Television was awash in such family-friendly fare as "Lassie," "Howdy Doody," "The Mickey Mouse Club," "The Donna Reed Show," and "The Adventures of Ozzie and Harriet."[2]

By contrast, American society conveyed a far different attitude toward children and parents in and around 1977. A top-selling book was titled *Our Selves, Our Children* (by the Boston Women's Health Book Collective) with the word order reflecting certain priorities. Between 1970 and 1981 Walt Disney Studios produced only one animated feature (*The Rescuers*) and actually laid off animators and cartoonists—a first for the company. Meanwhile, top-grossing films included such titles as *Omen II*, *Taxi Driver*, and the *Halloween* series. Children and teens were depicted as demonically possessed and incorrigibly wicked. In California, the passage of Proposition 13 froze property taxes, the prime source of public-school revenues. As similar tax revolts spread on state and local levels, school funding leveled off, then fell behind the rising cost of education.

Is childhood itself expanding or shrinking? That is, are the lines between the worlds of children and adults clarifying or blurring? When the lines grow sharper, child labor laws are enacted or enforced, truancy drops, teaching rises in esteem, and criminal acts or accidents involving children are seen as intrinsically evil or deplorably tragic. The cost of this sharpening includes strong pressures for conformity and often a high degree of emotional repression.

By contrast, in other periods adults are concerned that children's experiences not be too walled off from "real life." Consequently, structured education is de-emphasized in favor of spontaneity and exploration. Individuality is valued, and cultural creativity flowers in new forms of art, literature, and music. But the cost of this blurring for children has usually included rising truancy, coarsening manners, and crumbling schools.

Congregations treat children differently in various eras as well. If the number of square feet devoted to children and youth in a church building is growing and the portion of the church budget relating to children and youth is rising, a valuing of the new generation is evident. If the books and toys are relatively old and the variety of materials and equipment for children is shrinking, a different message is conveyed.

Congregations of the Protestant mainline of the 1950s built educational wings, added gymnasiums, and bought cribs, diaper pails, and closely graded denominational curricula for young families with children. Civic adults valued tradition, consensus, hierarchy, and loyalty, and expressed their faith as duty. But the Idealist youth in such a season increasingly feel smothered by conformity. They grow uneasy with a by-the-numbers rote faith of formulas and head knowledge.

By contrast, in the 1970s many of these mainline congregations were still using the same church-basement education rooms and toys—and sometimes even the same teachers. And the congregations were struggling to answer the question "Where are all the young families?" Those young families were headed by a generation of Adaptive parents who increasingly valued choices, options, spiritual exploration, and experience. Conveying a fixed set of traditions to youth was regarded by these parents as oppressive and stifling.

Schooling

Beyond parents and faith, children experience another significant impact on their formative lives: they go to school. Adult attitudes toward children often register in community actions regarding schools. At one end point of a pendulum swing (around 1947, for example) adults build schools, honor teachers, and support administrators. Adult expectations of students are objective, clear, and high. Children are seen as needing knowledge and preparation for adulthood. Individual achievement is expected and rewarded, and adults assume that their children will be as cooperative and collaborative as they themselves were.

At the other endpoint of the swing (around 1983, for example), schools are physically neglected, teachers are denigrated, and administrators face shrinking budgets. Adult expectations of students revolve around subjective criteria and self-esteem issues. Children are seen as needing relational skills as part of a core curriculum. Self-esteem and self-exploration are valued; cultural diversity and alternative viewpoints are honored in the classroom. Traditional academic achievement is either downplayed or, more disturbingly, actively sabotaged by student peers.

When the pendulum is swinging from strictness toward freedom, the result is a slow crumbling of expectations, a draining of the talent pool of teachers, and a plateauing (then a decline) in school funding. This season sees a revolt against structure in a child's world. Increasingly children are seen as bundles of creativity, full of fresh, unsullied insights, ready to teach the world.

When the pendulum swings from freedom toward strictness, schools are physically refurbished and brought up to new academic standards. Teaching gains importance and prestige. In such times the freedom bordering on anarchy in children's lives is now looked upon as threatening. Since children are seen as lacking character and morals, sets of rules and rising expectations are imposed. Schools are increasingly expected not only to convey knowledge, but also to improve character and to instill values of good citizenship. Such a set of imposed values tends to suppress individuality and creativity in favor of communal norms and a standardized sameness.

Coming of Age

As individuals of a generation grow toward adulthood, a number of transitional markers signal the coming stage of life. In earlier times, apprenticeships and indentured servitude terms ran out. In the 20th and 21st centuries a series of graduations have punctuated the completion of high school, vocational-technical training, and trade school. Those going on to higher education have prolonged the stage of youth through college and even postgraduate levels of education. Young people acquire driver's licenses, become eligible to vote, gain the right to enter into binding contracts, and reach the age at which they can legally buy and consume alcohol. Upon reaching the age of majority they acquire the full rights and duties of citizenship.

As generations move fully into adolescence and beyond, the adult generations begin to take notice. Many attitudes and expectations toward this generation are now conveyed to them, and the young generation notices the attention. Again a fourfold pattern emerges.

In one era adults show intense interest in the new Idealist young people, coupled with a certain smiling indulgence of their views, attitudes, and actions. Bad behaviors are met with understanding and forgiveness rather than with punishment. Youth are encouraged to find and express themselves; their individuality is celebrated.

In another period adults admire Civic youth as clean-cut, cooperative achievers. They regard youth as wonder kids, capable and mature beyond their years. Any miscreants are quickly separated out (to avoid contamination), and stern measures are taken to reform them, with a view toward reinserting them into a mainstream regarded as wholesome, positive, and virtuous.

In a third era adults view youth as a drag on society, useless and even dangerous. Nomad children have been told from their early days, "You're on your own, kid." Such a dispiriting message often causes members of a rising generation to be regarded, and to regard themselves, as cynical, hardened, stupid, and menacing.

In a final era adults see the new crop of youth as overly refined and deferential, socially timid. Adults wonder whether this Adaptive generation will ever really grow up and be worthy of responsibility. In response, these youth set out to prove their maturity, ability, and indispensability, earnestly and politely striving to show their worth.

Every generation does show its worth, but by different measures. As youth of a generation become adults, the assumptions made about them by older adults and the values instilled in them have formed a certain generational type. This type repeats the values and assumptions seen about 90 or 95 years earlier when the same generational type was at the same point in the life cycle. As the newest adults in society, they begin applying their values to the adult world. Forces in that adult world will continue to form their generational persona. Chapter 2 will trace the impact of these forces.

A GENERATION FINDS ITS VOICE

Strauss and Howe make a helpful distinction by dividing adulthood into three distinct life stages: rising adulthood, midlife, and elderhood. The most noticeable change between the first two stages is a shift from all sorts of *activity* in various settings to becoming *the leadership pool* for those settings. The transition is also marked by the more subtle change from *testing* values in rising adulthood (ages 22–44) to *applying* values in midlife (ages 45–66).[1]

As a generation's members move through their 20s and into their 30s, they are recognized as adults by the rest of society. People in this life stage are expected to finish school, begin making a full-time contribution to the workforce, join the military, become adult consumers of goods and services, vote, serve on juries, date, marry, begin families, attend religious services, and contribute time, talent, and treasure to the support of congregations and charities.

Working

Economic forces shape a fresh generation of workers and consumers in this stage of life. New Adaptive adults are welcomed as full partners in the workplace. Job and career pathways are sharply defined; dedication and loyalty are expected and rewarded. Capital, labor, and government combine to build a great economic machine that produces goods and services at a stunning rate. Both poverty and great individual wealth shrink as the middle class expands through a combination of high growth, high wages, high productivity, stable prices, and public policies that encourage a broad distribution of wealth. The post–World War II boom is the most recent example of such an era.

A second era features a disruption of this machine. A new generation of Idealist adults considers dutiful and repetitive work personally unfulfilling.

The Idealists' sense of individuality leads them to demand work that is meaningful, and renders them suspicious of large organizations. While this behavior opens up niches for smaller organizations and innovative start-ups, it also leaves the economy unable to cope with economic shocks. Such unexpected events as minor wars, a bank panic, or an oil embargo derail the machine. Large corporations stagger under the impact. Unemployment and inflation rates swing widely, policy-makers argue, and a dark cloud settles over the economy.

A third type of era presents Nomad young adults with an economic landscape that requires risk-taking and offers little job security. Large organizations and corporations are disdained as lumbering dinosaurs while entrepreneurs are widely admired. A lucky few strike it immensely rich. In contrast to the situation in the first era, the middle class shrinks as the gap between rich and poor widens into a canyon. Individual résumés brim with variety and shorter job tenures as lifetime careers disappear but new opportunities appear.

The fourth type of era has usually been marked by an economic crisis. A generation of new Civic adults enters a broken economy with high unemployment, low wages, and collapsing businesses. Far fewer are rich than in other eras, while many of the middle class fall into poverty. Public and private relief efforts provide basic needs of food, clothing, and shelter. Many members of the new working generation are pulled into government-financed and privately funded programs that teach skills while building or repairing public works.

Marriage and Parenting

Rising adulthood is the stage at which social pressures relating to marriage reach their peak. One era finds Adaptive young people, stung by older adults' expressed doubts about their maturity, reacting by marrying at earlier and earlier ages to prove their adulthood. In particular, women of such a generation seek marriage as a path to security.

Another era finds dating and marriage rituals helter-skelter, with no agreed-upon conventions or expectations. Rising adult Nomads in such eras are forced to construct patterns and invent rituals for connecting and for creating a life together. They were children and teens during times of upheaval in their parents' marriages and are determined to avoid repeating their parents' mistakes. They seek counseling and advice on marriage and family so that their marriages will be more durable than the ones they saw fall apart in their youth.

Another era finds Idealist adults stressing individuality and iconoclasm. Personal relationships are tentative as individuals value and guard their individuality. Freedom and being true to oneself outrank commitment and loyalty to others. Extended singleness becomes common, divorce rates spike, and single-parent households become widespread. Some women of such a generation view marriage as a prison, damaging to their personhood. Such generations produce a significant number of women who never marry.

By contrast, another era displays commitments and relationships as the norm and the desire of both men and women. Such times find elders encouraging and expecting rising Civic adults to meet and commit to one another. In such eras singleness is seen as preliminary to marriage, or as aberrant. Generations formed in such times disparage divorce, and seek out or arrange mates for the widowed.

People in their 20s and 30s produce children and take on the responsibilities of parenthood. Two factors bear on a generation's child rearing. First, each generational type tends to react against the parenting it received. So, for instance, Nomads react to what they felt was the randomness and underprotection of their youth by increasing order and protection for their children. Adaptives who felt their childhood days were overprotected and emotionally stifling increasingly raise their children with more opportunities for risk and emotional exploration.

Second, rising adult parents look up the age ladder and see the generation ahead of them parenting older children and teens. This older set of parents (usually passing from rising adulthood into midlife) influences parenting styles, choices, and outlooks. Sometimes the new parents adopt and amplify patterns laid down by the next-elder parent generation. In the 1980s and 1990s Generation X parents followed the lead of Boomer parents by attempting to increase the safety of children's lives. Boomers led the way in enacting child seat-belt laws and bicycle helmet regulations. Generation X parents surfed the Internet for choices in crib liner pads, and designed software filters to protect children from cyberporn Web sites.

At other times new parents in rising adulthood resist and reverse the influence of these next-elder parent choices. The first decade of the 1900s saw a strong upsurge in support of child labor laws, stronger enforcement of school truancy rules, and the beginnings of the school milk monitor programs. These were all reversals of 1890s conditions, when runaways were tolerated, child workers were maimed in factories, and newsboys hawked papers on street corners to supplement family incomes.

Religious Changes

As a generation moves into rising adulthood, the American religious landscape shows widely differing terrain. One era finds religious leaders encouraging spiritual exploration, experimentation, and separation into communal groups. Rising adult Idealists establish new movements and splinter groups with intense spiritual energy and claims upon their members. Most American adults will recognize and remember such ferment in the 1960s and 1970s. Various Eastern maharishis appeared, transcendental meditation beckoned as a life pattern, and Islam first stirred into an African American form. More darkly, such an era also sees more cultic movements such as the Rev. Jim Jones's People's Temple, with its shocking mass suicide/murder. Charges of brainwashing were lodged against followers of the Rev. Sun Myung Moon and his Unification Church.

But other generations in this stage of life find a profoundly different religious landscape. Adaptive generations see a broad religious consensus in most communities, with differences downplayed and nearly all religious groups undergirding a common civic religion that can swing toward unabashed nationalism. Americans now drawing Social Security can remember a period of such consensus after World War II. Mainline Protestant bodies dominated most communities and cut a wide swath on the new television networks. The Rev. Billy Graham's crusades brought masses of heretofore shunned evangelicals under an American nationalist umbrella.

Civic generations in rising adulthood encounter yet another landscape in American religious life. Social structures are twisted and strained by history-altering events. Economic hard times grind parishioners down as careers are shattered, jobs are scarce, and daily survival looms as a challenge. Congregations in such times become beacons of hope and sources of practical comfort. In the 1860s Southern congregations cared for the convalescing Confederate wounded and donated the metal of church bells to cannon foundries.[2] Southern preachers approved the course of the war in Virginia, comparing the Southern Jefferson Davis and the Northern Abraham Lincoln to Israel's southern kingdom under King Hezekiah holding off the fearsome northern barbarian King Sennacherib.[3]

Denominational differences are submerged, papered over, or simply dismissed outright in the face of the secular emergency. With the outbreak of World War II, the Wisconsin Evangelical Lutheran Synod offered to provide chaplains to the U.S. military, on the condition that they would minister only to WELS members. The military responded that it was accepting only chaplains who were Protestant, Catholic, or Jewish, and in any case the congregations would all be in olive drab.[4]

Finally, Nomad generations come into adulthood finding diversity, openness, and tolerance to be the broad religious watchwords, while various truth claims blare across the landscape. Under the mantle of openness and toleration, more intolerant and sectarian groups attract attention. Those moderating the religious discussion in these times and defending every group's contribution to the discussion are often bewildered and perplexed by groups that are strident and exclusive. So in the 1980s first the Moral Majority and then the Christian Coalition pursued fundamentalist aims while promoting themselves as another option. The diversity-and-tolerance-promoting People for the American Way found themselves hard-pressed to exclude or deny a place in the discussion to such groups without undercutting their own principles.

Toward Midlife

When individuals pass from youth into adulthood, a host of visible social markers signal the transition (driver's license, graduation, end of apprenticeship, for example). By contrast there are few outward markers as adults age into their middle 40s and enter a new stage of life. They attend 20-year and quarter-century class reunions. Women approach or reach menopause. Adults find themselves raising teenagers rather than small children. Many individuals undergo what has been termed a midlife crisis. Some struggle to hold on to (or return to) an ever more distant youth. They divorce, marry a "trophy" wife, or have an affair. They change careers, relocate, change religious congregations, begin or stop attending worship services, all the while haunted by the feeling that this may be their last chance to make a major change of direction.

Midlife has often been the time when aging parents die and inheritances arrive. Such estates have sometimes financed a middle-age fling but more often have sobered a generation conscious of moving up a notch. Now no older generation stands between oneself and old age and death. This sort of reevaluation signals the crossing into midlife.

CHAPTER 3

A GENERATION MAKES ITS MARK

A subtle but significant change happens as a generation's members move into their mid-40s and beyond. Until now adulthood has been dominated by *activity*—professionally, socially, politically, and within the family. Younger adults have been testing the values of their youth, discarding some and refining or enhancing still others.

The Age of Leadership

But as a generation's members reach age 44, they move into a new stage of life that will last into their mid-60s. People achieve that unique combination of education, experience, savvy, and well-paced energy that moves them into positions of real *leadership*, the key activity from one's mid-40s to mid-60s. Society and institutions have no one else to turn to: other generations are too young and inexperienced, or so old that they have already had their turn, and often lack numbers, health, energy, interest, or perhaps credibility.

Since 1789 there have been 43 U.S. presidents—35 initially gaining the office by election, and four others (Theodore Roosevelt, Coolidge, Truman, and Lyndon Johnson) elected in their own right after assuming the office from the vice presidency upon the death of a president. Of these 39 all but two (Kennedy and Reagan) were, when elected, between 44 and 66 years of age, the leadership stage of life. (Indeed, there was a great deal of public rumbling about both Kennedy's youth and Reagan's age impinging upon their fitness for the job—backhanded evidence of the boundaries of this stage of life and its primary task.)

Strauss and Howe observe that history shapes generations, but they also note that as a generation crosses into midlife, we see evidence of another truth—generations shape history. Clearly not every person is gifted with leadership abilities, but it is at this stage of life that individuals assume leadership. They are no longer seen as rising stars or young wonders. They make partner, become senior pastor, gain a seat on the board, or are named president, director, bishop, dean, or CEO. As leaders and elders a generation's impact on younger and future generations is vast. Because a different generation fills the midlife role every 22 years or so, parental attitudes shift; and business, labor, and government collaborate differently. A new generation of leaders restructures institutions to express different values. As such leaders decide what sort of books will be published, which movies made, and what stories covered and run in the popular press, what is regarded as culturally acceptable changes.

Idealist generations bring a visionary character to leadership. They easily think "outside the box," and question standing assumptions and social or institutional rules. (In this life stage they are in a position to make wholesale changes in such assumptions and rules.) Idealist leaders, more than other generational types, are willing to explore and implement fundamental changes in institutions. They understand that such a paradigm shift can touch off controversy and argument, but these leaders seem more content than other leaders to endure such fury. Indeed, these leaders are often willing to provoke such contention in the first place for the sake of bringing on what they see as needed change.

In the secular realm Steve Jobs of Apple Computer typified such leadership. He moved computers out of climate-controlled rooms guarded by technicians using machine code. Now computers like his groundbreaking Macintosh and successor models like the iMac are on desktops, usable by anyone who can manipulate a computer mouse.

Religious Leaders

On the religious side, Idealist leaders across the ages dream dreams and see visions. They glimpse a different and compelling vision of the world. They labor to translate what they have seen and heard into descriptions and directions for those whom they lead. When Puritan John Winthrop arrived at the Massachusetts Bay Colony in 1630 and saw the rude huts of a muddy settlement, he nonetheless exclaimed, "I see a shining city on a hill!"[1]

In contrast with this inward focus, the Civic generational type shows its leadership persona by altering the outer world. Business, labor, and government bodies work together as a mighty force. Canal systems are built, or railroads are extended across prairies and mountains, or millions of cubic feet of concrete are poured to build interstate highways and airport complexes. Older housing stock is torn down and replaced by clean but repetitive designs, whether Old West street fronts or brownstone row houses.

As religious leaders and members, such a generation expresses its faith through good works. Leaders emphasize the importance of faith in action, leaving them prone to a works-righteousness view of the faith, rather like New England cleric Benjamin Colman in the early 1700s exhorting his parishioners to "Be up and doing. Activity. Activity."[2] Congregational members set records for worship attendance. The generational propensity for building also shows up in religious circles. In the 1940s and 1950s denominational bodies planted new congregations, providing financial support for churches to build using a limited number of blueprints.

People of the Adaptive generational type do not do much physical construction, but rather build human relationships and connections, seeking to help individuals grow emotionally, spiritually, and relationally. Such generations produce, honor, and encourage therapists, counselors, pastors, rabbis, and various helping professions and roles. Adaptives have a touching faith in the improvability of the human condition. Members of such a generation stood in lines stretching for city blocks for tickets to hear psychiatric pioneer Sigmund Freud on tour in 1909.[3] Their quiet-spoken abolition societies of the 1820s brought a legal end to slavery in the Northern states and brought the question to serious discussion in Virginia.[4]

In church circles, Clinical Pastoral Education is first made an option, then a requirement of many a seminary curriculum. Adaptives push through the ordination of women in mainline denominations, make churchwide apologies for prior sins and transgressions, and, like Unitarianism's founder William Channing in the early 1800s, look for the divine spark in each human being—whom they see as basically good.[5]

The Nomad type of leadership is enterprising, entrepreneurial, risk-taking, and rule-breaking. Nomads are often comfortable with newer technology. Such a generational type moved information at the speed of light and goods faster than a horse could run for the first time in human history in the 1840s (telegraph and railroads). Nomads pragmatically bend or break rules to survive. Despite the 18th century rules of war, Washington campaigned in winter, his soldiers marching with feet wrapped in rags; he crossed the uncrossable Delaware River, and captured the German mercenaries at Trenton, New Jersey.

In religious bodies Nomads form functional alliances for local social-ministry efforts across denominational lines. They show a renewed interest in denominational traditions, having come late to their faith but often thirsty for all the riches a religious body can offer. Yet they seldom allow those traditions to interfere with a pragmatic response to emergencies. So during a battle in the American Revolution, the Rev. James Caldwell, chaplain to a New Jersey regiment in Washington's army, found his soldiers running out of paper wadding for their muskets. Caldwell burst into a nearby church and scooped up armloads of hymnals. Instructing his men to rip up the hymnals and use the pages for wadding, he pointed to the British and growled that the men should load their muskets and "Give 'em Watts!"—a reference to the prolific and much-published hymn writer Isaac Watts.[6]

A generation in midlife makes its most telling marks on social institutions by implementing the values of its leaders. Its successes and failures shape the final stage of life a generation faces in elderhood.

CHAPTER 4

THE GRAYING
OF A GENERATION

As members of a generation age into their middle 60s and beyond, they cross one more boundary between stages of life. This transition from midlife to elderhood has a number of social markers that draw a line between older and younger adults.

Seniors often change their living arrangements to mark the transition, sometimes by moving in with younger relatives, at other times moving to be with their peers. In past times as income sources changed or even disappeared, older people were often economically dependent on younger family members. In the past half-century or so the move into retirement has been marked by relocation, making Florida not only one of the fastest-growing of the 50 states, but giving it both the highest median age (36.2) and the highest percentage of population over age 65 (18.3 percent).[1]

Of course, in earlier centuries people often worked until they were physically unable to do so, with precious little time or opportunity to enjoy anything like the modern idea of retirement. (And it *is* a modern idea. Prussian Chancellor Otto von Bismarck instituted the first national retirement pension plan in the 1880s. An able politician, he co-opted an idea of his opponents and kept it cheap, setting the eligibility age at 65 in a day when few workers lived past 50.)

Most people at the dawn of the 21st century, looking back two millennia to Rome, are unaware that archeologists generally agree that the average life expectancy in the Roman Empire was a mere 36 years. Physical maturity came late in one's teens, and death came rather soon after to most. Only a few lived long enough for their hair to turn white. The blessing from Psalm 128, "May you see your children's children," takes on deeper meaning in light of this short life span.

Perhaps nearly as startling was the average American life expectancy in 1900—46 years. Improved health care, better nutrition, and the widespread use of labor-saving machinery have only recently combined to raise American life expectancy for most individuals to the biblical three score years and ten, and beyond. To be sure, wise old heads (and old fools) have been known from ancient times, and their influence and impact have been strong. Younger generations considered the wisdom and experience of these rare elders and often showed them deference and honor.

As each of the four generational types in turn reaches elderhood, each brings a lifetime of accomplishments and failures. All the younger generations looking to the top of the age ladder find the newest generation of elders remaking society's assumptions of the aged. Consider the contrast between seniors of 1964 and of 1985.

In 1964 members of the Lost generation of Nomads ranged in age from 64 to 81. They voted Republican, favored small government, and expected no special favors for themselves. Many spoke a polyglot of "old country" languages; they lived in a wide range of housing arrangements, depending on their retirement incomes, and many lived in poverty. Younger generations then viewed old people as crusty, cantankerous, and often isolated. Elders were politically insignificant and mostly ignored by business and advertising.[2]

By 1985 the American view of elders had been totally transformed by the presence of the World War II GI generation of Civics in retirement (born 1901–1924). These seniors voted Democratic and enjoyed many federal programs favoring people over 65. The 89th Congress of 1964–1965, composed of 70 percent GIs, took care of the GI generation's coming geriatric medical needs by enacting Medicare. (In this book, I will usually use "GI" to refer to this generation as a whole, not only to those who served in the armed forces.) In the early 1970s this dominant generation added automatic cost-of-living escalators to Social Security. Sun City–type retirement communities mushroomed across the Sunbelt, filled with energetic seniors who played golf and shuffleboard, swam laps, and provided some of their own community security, using motorized golf carts.[3]

Younger members of society now viewed senior citizens as a powerful interest group. The elders were the Gray Panthers, quick to mobilize political pressure against any politician who dared to suggest changes in Social Security. The AARP (formerly the American Association of Retired Persons) became one of the most powerful lobby groups in Washington. For even saying aloud that perhaps some day Social Security benefits might have to be restrained in some way, Rep. Dan Rostenkowski, chairman of the powerful House Ways and Means Committee, was chased down the Chicago streets by angry senior women proclaiming, "How dare you!"[4]

Elders as Seen by Younger People

Idealist generations in elderhood are honored by those younger—revered
and even held in awe. They are seen as brooding and wise, expecting and
generally getting respect and deference from younger generations. They
leave a legacy of unflinching purpose, visionary ideals, and a willingness to
sacrifice to the point of martyrdom. Benjamin Franklin, hearing John
Hancock say at the signing of the Declaration of Independence, "We shall
all hang together," noted wryly as he signed, "Most assuredly, or we shall
all hang separately."[5] His generation's visions of independence, a democratic
republic, economic opportunity, and religious freedom, embodied in the
Constitution, still are key ingredients in the American experiment two
centuries later.

In religious circles Idealist generations embody a faith's ideals.
Personally austere, they provide a high moral tone, deep spirituality, and
approval of religious fervor deep into their old age. They resemble Moses
or the other prophets, willing both to critique the current immorality, and to
describe a promised land that lies not far ahead.

Members of Nomad generations, after a lifetime of risk-taking and
adventure, are often left bruised and beaten by life. They seek to protect
younger generations from life's dangers, warning against hazards. They
seek stability and safety for younger generations, but are usually hooted
down as out-of-touch old codgers. Civics of the next-younger generation
have commonly ignored such seniors or ridiculed them as "old fogies" and
"stick-in-the-muds."

Nomads leave a legacy of worldly realism and practicality. Their few
spectacular economic winners can use wealth to make up for a spotty
educational record by providing better opportunities for younger generations.
Libraries built with generous gifts from Andrew Carnegie in the small towns
and big cities of America gave millions a chance to read books they may
otherwise never have encountered. John and Abigail Rockefeller's
underwriting of the restoration of Williamsburg has inspired thousands of
Americans to study their national history and ponder the wisdom of the
Revolutionary leaders and thinkers.

In congregations members of the Nomad generational type are the
sturdy defenders of the faith tradition. Even when younger generations
would like to gloss over the darker sides of a faith tradition (for example,
Martin Luther's excoriation of the Jews, or the hangings of Quakers in
Puritan New England), this generation insists that these be faced.

There is a hint of Israel's high priest Eli to this generation in elderhood. Eli as ruler of Israel (1 Samuel 1–4) had made a working accommodation with the surrounding Philistines, providing Israel with a precarious security. He first growled at Hannah, but upon hearing her story became solicitous toward her. Later he showed true kindness toward the boy prophet Samuel. Tormented by his sons' sinfulness and blinded by great age, he despaired that his own sons ignored his warnings and brought ruin.

The Civic generational type brings energy to this stage of life, a vigor that is usually invested in fellow members of the generation. As a generation, Civics have conquered in war and flourished in peace, building infrastructure and prosperity, spreading wealth more evenly than any other generational type. Younger generations see them as quick to defend their own generation's public rewards, whether land grants to Revolutionary War veterans, or state and federal pensions for Civil War veterans.

In the religious field this generational type continues to show a propensity for outward good works in the life of faith. Civics can become frustrated as their capacity for large-scale good deeds wanes. Suspicious of or repelled by inner religious passion, they often also miss the comforts of a passionate faith. They can grow miffed if they believe they are often asked for congregational financial support but seldom asked for wisdom or shown the respect they themselves showed their own elders decades before.

They age as King David aged. Civic generations look back on their communal power facing a crisis, as David united the 12 tribes of Jacob into a single nation (2 Samuel 1–10). They are bewildered when their children (like Absalom) rise in rebellion and protest, attacking the very constructions (a united kingdom; worship centered in Jerusalem) that are markers of the eldest generation's power (2 Samuel 13–18).

Finally, Adaptive generations move into elderhood economically secured by a host of mostly private funding sources. (The first widespread industrial pension plans began amassing funds around 1910.[6]) Having often played life safe in their earlier years, this generation of seniors enjoys new experiences and careful thrills. (Even though former president George H. W. Bush is a GI-generation Civic, his septuagenarian sky-diving with a dozen Secret Service agents in the air alongside and on the ground for support is Adaptive-style calibrated excitement.)

There is an air of the aged Solomon in Adaptive generations. They are people who adorn life with art (average age for an opera patron in the 1990s was 62[7]) and collect and index information ("These are the sayings of Agur, son of Jakeh, which Solomon also caused to be written" [Prov. 30:1 RSV].) They are sensitive to the emotional, religious, and economic pressures among younger generations and often seek to mediate between them. ("Yet for the sake of your father David I will not tear [the kingdom] from you in your lifetime" [2 Kings 11:12].)

Younger generations looking up at Adaptives in elderhood see kind, warm-hearted people who worry about many small issues and try to avoid being a burden. Currently the Silent generation has cooled the debate about Social Security (no more congressmen are being chased down the streets), while funding their own retirements with 401(k)s, IRAs, Keoghs, and other pension plans. Often the more affluent among them form the huge flocks of congregational snowbirds who mass their numbers in Sunbelt congregations during the winter, and in the North for the summer months.

Grandchildren

As a rule one's grandchildren are of the same generational type as the grandparents. The two age groups have different life experiences, to be sure, but both were raised by parents who shared a generational type.

The similarity in parenting assumptions accounts in part for the strong grandparent-grandchild bond, since both are of the same generational type. In the final years of a generation, this reappearance of this type can offer comfort and consolation to members of a generation.

For three of the four types this turn of the cycle is a comfort. The exception is the Nomad generational type, a group that had to grow up fast in a world that was not friendly to children. Such a generation in elderhood is saddened to see such attitudes appearing again, and its members are frustrated at not being able to make much of a difference. Still, this gruff generation often takes pains on an individual level to offer kindness, understanding, and protection.

Death and Dying

As generations reach elderhood, their members begin dying. How does a given generation face death? Members of Idealist generations can often experience faith deep in their bones. They see death as a transition to a higher plane. They are often content to die, comforted by the promises of their faith, and knowing that they leave behind a better world, thanks to their idealistic efforts.

Nomad generations see death differently. There can be a very quiet, almost resigned quality to this final life passage. Many of this type want only to leave with a bit of quiet dignity. Religious themes of rest and peace have a poignant appeal for many who have seen some the harsher realities of life.

Adaptive generations find death and the rites surrounding it as one last opportunity for modifying conventions with choices and changes that will ease the pain of those left behind. As members of the current Adaptive generation of Silents have begun dying, their funerals and memorial services have featured more cremations and rites drawn from eclectic sources.

By contrast, Civic generations embrace conventions and traditions wholeheartedly. They may spare no expense in these final rites of passage, an extravagance often noted by mourners who attend these funerals. In the 1730s the state of Massachusetts passed a law to curb the funeral excesses of the dying Glorious generation war veterans.[8]

Every generation moves through the four stages of life outlined in these opening four chapters. Clusters of traits appear and show themselves on many fronts, and coalesce into four generational types. It is now time to sort out the clusters and trace the generational biographies of each type.

GENERATIONAL BIOGRAPHIES

The next four chapters will be devoted to biographies of each of the four generational types. Everyone is a member of a generational type, and knows some of his or her own generation's story. But often one's knowledge of another generation's story is spotty or unbalanced. These chapters attempt to give an idea of what it's like to live within another generational type to help all generations understand one another.

Within each chapter, references to the other three generational types will be minimal, except as other generations directly affect the story of the generation under discussion. Interactions between generations will be the prime focus of chapters 9 through 12. The major exception will be child rearing, by definition an intergenerational process.

ACCENTUATE THE FLEXIBLE

We will first trace the generational type Strauss and Howe call "Adaptive." Since the 1600s the Adaptive type has appeared several times (as has each of the other three types). Within the Adaptive type, Strauss and Howe have identified the following generations and their birth years, and have given each a name.

ADAPTIVE GENERATIONS

Birth Years	Name used by Straus & Howe
1925-1942	Silents
1843-1859	Progressives
1767-1791	Compromisers
1674-1700	Enlighteners

Youth

The years 1925–1942 saw the birth of America's latest Adaptive generation, the first since before the Civil War. Adaptives are children in times of technological progress, economic upheaval, and political crisis. Children born in the 1840s and 1850s (the Progressives) saw adults adjust to long-distance communication and transportation technologies (telegraph and railroads) and face financial panics (1857). Such children overheard an increasingly bitter and violent debate over slavery.

Similarly for children of the 1925–1942 years, coast-to-coast telephone calls became possible, autos sold by the millions, and the fledgling airlines welcomed their first passengers. The economic and social frenzy of the 1920s ended with a thud in 1929 as the Great Depression began. These Adaptive generation children and teens overheard frightened adults bitterly debating issues surrounding labor unions, the role of government, capitalism, and foreign wars.

In such tumultuous eras churches stress the fundamentals of the faith, becoming sources of comfort and mutual support. Worship forms follow denominational norms, and a great deal of energy and time is spent on providing practical relief and assistance.

During the formative years of the Silent generation, churches opened orphanages, schools, and nursing homes for the aged. Cross-denominational efforts provided a division of labor in communities as, for instance, one congregation ran a soup kitchen, while another's parish nurse provided basic medical care, and a third provided sleeping quarters for drifters and for families who had lost their homes. Doctrinal differences were papered over and seen as less important in the face of the Depression and World War II.

During such upheavals adults in the exhausting struggle for daily survival often act as though emotional nuances and subtlety are luxuries for themselves. But as children in such times, Adaptive generations are left free to explore human emotions and work through relationships. They acquire a rich understanding of the range and depth of this part of humanity— a lifelong mark of Adaptive generations.

Beginning in 1942 local draft boards from every community inducted hundreds, even thousands, of young men into the military (and the not-so-young—some 40-year-olds were drafted) Ultimately 15 million GI generation men (born 1901–1924, just ahead of the Adaptives) went into uniform, while most of the rest went to work in the war effort, finally ending the Depression.

As so many men disappeared from public view and home life, one side effect was that an unusually high ratio of women were left nurturing the maturing Adaptive (Silent) generation. These women often found their economic situation stabilized, even improved, as the fears of the Depression receded. Traditional female attributes of warmth, listening and social skills, sympathy, support, and self-effacement were all powerfully exemplified for these Adaptives. This nurturing, often lacking the balance of the usual male presence, reinforced the Silents' childhood explorations in the area of human relations and cemented their generational character.

This sensitivity and warmth ran counter to some of the darker social currents of their youth. The young Silents saw discrimination and prejudice in the war years as American citizens of Japanese descent were forcibly removed from their homes and resettled in internment camps, and the armed forces continued to segregate the races and to exclude or limit black units' participation in combat or skilled job assignments. The Silents' youthful sense of fair play and sympathy was awakened. They remembered these injustices and sought to change them when their turn at leadership came.

The Silents also saw breakthroughs and hope for the oppressed. The 442nd Rainbow Division, composed of draft-age Japanese Americans, fought with distinction. The Black Panther tank brigade, made up of African Americans, spearheaded General George Patton's famed Third Army and liberated the first Nazi death camps. Women on the home front worked jobs once reserved for men, as exemplified in the character "Rosie the Riveter." The Silents remembered these models and possibilities.

As Adaptive generations head for adulthood, the national crisis peaks and resolves. Adults fight wars, repair the economy, and achieve national goals. Social unity for the sake of such goals overrides the value of human relationships, so minority groups and Adaptive generation children and teens are expected to stay in line and be polite, deferential, and appreciative. This pressure for conformity accounts for part of the bond Adaptive generations have felt for minorities, and has made Adaptive generations in their adult years champions of minority groups.

Members of the 20th century's Adaptive generation like Colin Powell, Sandra Day O'Connor, and Phil Donahue collected aluminum door-to door for the war effort, studied silhouettes of enemy aircraft, and stayed out of trouble. A 1943 survey of Texas teachers listed the two major high-school discipline problems as excessive gum chewing and cutting in line.[1] These youngsters cheered every Allied advance, saw the dread in adults' faces at the approach of a Western Union telegraph messenger, and lined the streets to welcome the returning GIs in 1945. It may have occurred to some of those on the curbstones that they had just missed out on something big.

Rising Adulthood

Demobilizing GIs encountered the leading edge of this sensitive and deferential Adaptive generation at colleges and in job-application lines. The confident, war-winning GIs were quick to collect society's thanks in the form of veterans' preferences in hiring, the GI bill for college education, and VA (Veterans Administration) loans for mortgages. Particularly the late-wave GIs (born in the years just before 1925) used these advantages to elbow aside polite and slightly awestruck Adaptives in dating, college enrollments, and jobs. These earnest and careful Adaptives struck the GIs as tentative and unassuming, far different from their officers in the military. GI generation historian William Manchester called these kids the "Silent generation," and the name stuck.[2]

Stung by GI condescension, many of the Silents moved quickly to prove their maturity. High-school girls learned to drive. Boys and girls went steady, exchanged pins, and got married at ever younger ages (The average marrying age for both men and women reached an all-time low in 1955—23 for men and 20 for women.[3])

Women like Grace Kelly and Jacqueline Bouvier showed the way by waiting and knowing that "Our day will come/and we'll have everything"[4]—and their handsome princes (Rainier and Kennedy) arrived to take them to their shining mansions. Millions moved into the suburbs to acquire tract houses, station wagons with wood-paneled sides, and the trappings of modernity.

But other Silents earnestly questioned the suburban tide sweeping the country. The "all together now!" cheeriness among their neighbors sounded like a version of the "take it or leave it, kid" talk they had heard from their elders a decade or two earlier. Some of these Silents labeled the new grid-patterned, GI-built suburbs "Squaresvilles," lamenting the boxy sameness of the houses "all made of ticky-tacky."[5] Some even refused to join the clean-cut, well-pressed, team-playing GI workforce by becoming part of the bearded, coffee-house-frequenting, bongo-playing Beat generation. Their thirst for other possibilities bloomed in the 1960s.

At home Silents who chafed under the conformity expected by mainline and civil religions watched new religious options flicker across their new television sets. They saw the Rev. Oral Roberts bring sawdust-trail revivalism into American living rooms. They also listened thoughtfully as Bishop Fulton Sheen patiently explained the features of Roman Catholicism to a Protestant-dominated church culture. They cheered, admired, and helped elect the handsome Roman Catholic John Kennedy to the presidency, and delighted in the changes and opportunities Vatican II opened for Catholics.

The rising generation of Silents stuck to their books, becoming the most credentialed generation in American history. Despite the GIs' head start, the Silents' education served them well in landing jobs and starting careers in the great American economic machine that roared to life in 1946. Members of the Silent generation were in demand as advisors, assistants, junior partners, aides, and helpers of all kinds. Their relatively small numbers kept them in demand throughout the labor force. The corporations for which the Silents worked laid career paths that rewarded loyalty with seniority, fringe benefits, annual pay raises, and the promise of the corner office—if you persevered and were white and male.

This white-and-male assumption gnawed at the rising Adaptives, who saw the postwar effort to force women back into homemaking, and blacks back under the thumb of "Jim Crow" laws and customs. Silents began asking why these sorts of moves were needed in peacetime after women and minorities had helped mightily in wartime. A tired GI generation seamstress and a young Silent generation preacher (Rosa Parks and the Rev. Martin Luther King, Jr.), started a boycott in 1955 that showed the Birmingham, Alabama, bus system that discrimination could be a losing idea.

As the 1960s arrived, this Adaptive generation's archetypal traits regarding human relations and fairness emerged more sharply. In a soft-spoken reaction to their exacting childhoods, they began multiplying options and choices in all human fields. Starting with the nonviolent, massed efforts of Martin Luther King, white Freedom Riders spent their summer vacations from college riding buses across the South. Called outside agitators, communists, and worse, white Silents of conscience joined ranks with black Silent targets of segregation to make America live down its shame and live up to its ideals of humanity and equality. To this day, Silent leaders recount the historic experience of being with Dr. King at the Edmund Pettus Bridge or at the Lincoln Memorial for the "I Have a Dream" speech, or facing down hate in the South. These are their badges of honor, and their efforts are enshrined in the Voting Rights and Civil Rights Acts of 1964 and 1965, and in the 24th Amendment to the Constitution, which abolished the poll tax. The Silents' generational creed of humanity, fairness, and inclusiveness was being enacted.

Previous Adaptive generations have also moved to overcome race barriers. Richard Allen of the Compromiser generation found it demeaning to be segregated from white parishioners at St. George's Methodist church in New York. After many earnest conversations and efforts, Allen in 1792 became the founder of a new Methodist body, the African Methodist Episcopal (AME) Church. In addition to providing a spiritual home for his fellow blacks (and several whites), Allen and the newly launched denomination began working for economic uplift and social opportunities for African Americans during Washington's first term.[6] This crusade has ebbed and flowed, to be sure, but it has been part of the Republic from its beginning, thanks to the Adaptive type in the generational cycle.

In similar fashion, many of the Silent generation's early-marrying women found bridge clubs, tiki-torch patio parties, and the modern conveniences of housework stultifying. Pioneer feminist Betty Friedan's *The Feminine Mystique* (1963) gave words to this inchoate longing for something more, something like opportunity, equality, fairness, and choices. Gloria Steinem and her emulators of this Adaptive generation began calling for economic opportunities and the reshaping of gender-biased laws. This generation's political cadre did so as they entered statehouses across the country. From 1969 to 1975 the number of states with no-fault divorce laws went from 0 to 45.[7] In 1970 the California legislature considered a bill that would lower the permissible age for newspaper delivery girls to 10 (instead of 18), to match the age for newsboys.[8]

In religious bodies too, this generation opened opportunities and created options for women and minorities. In 1970, Silent generation delegates to national assemblies of the American Lutheran Church and the Lutheran Church in America voted to ordain women, and Episcopalians followed suit in 1976. Reform Judaism ordained Sally Priesand in 1972 as a rabbi, breaking an ancient precedent, and paving the way for Conservative Jews to follow suit with Amy Eilberg as their first female rabbi in 1985.[9]

These modern accomplishments parallel the achievements of earlier pioneers and minority breakthroughs in previous Adaptive generations. Progressive Anna Howard Shaw was ordained by the Methodist Protestant Church in 1880, though the idea did not spread widely. A Compromiser-controlled Maryland legislature made good an earlier religious lapse by extending full political rights to Jews in the state in 1826.[10]

Parenting and Schools

Adaptive generations have generally believed in fewer rules and less structure for children while encouraging and celebrating their individual traits. Exploring and celebrating their own individuality as adults, the Silent generation of parents has seen little harm in expanding such exploration for children. The darker side of this quest for personal options among Silent adults was an explosion in the divorce rate, causing a sharp rise in the number of children living with one parent, or a parent and a step-parent. Divorce lost much of its stigma and at times brought a merciful end to a bad marriage. In such cases the children were often left in a better situation. At other times divorce landed hard on the children, typified by the searing 1979 film *Kramer vs. Kramer*. In many of these cases the children of a warm, caring, and sensitive generation of Adaptives found that to survive the sharp edges of a bleak childhood they needed to become hardened, cool, and detached.

Adaptive generations tend to whittle down a school's core curriculum while adding specialists to the school staff who counsel, or teach art, music, dance, gym, home management, or shop. Rules mandating admission of previously excluded groups of people are promulgated and enforced, but also often resented. In the 1820s the Compromisers made broad efforts to encourage girls to become literate. The 1870s and 1880s saw a surge into schools, first of Negro children, then Indians, Mexican Americans, and immigrants from Europe and Asia. These moves of inclusivity touched off a predictable exclusionary backlash of segregated/private/parochial schools that evaded public mandates promoting mingling and integration. The 1896 Supreme Court decision in *Plessy v. Ferguson* that established the "separate but equal" concept (usually enforced as separate and unequal) was a signal victory for those resenting an Adaptive generational type's views.

Midlife

The Silent generation that sat at lunch counters and accomplished the integration of schools has marched most of the way through midlife, leaving an Adaptive stamp on leadership across society. The coming Boomers are only slowly displacing Silent leaders in social institutions, so Silent leadership traits are usually still the norm in many settings.

As economic, cultural, and religious leaders in midlife, Silents were still wary of anything that came across as arbitrary or demanding conformity. Instead, they sought to lead by consensus, valuing inclusivity and openness. People previously excluded because of race, gender, or disability are now welcomed. Mediating and communication skills rose in value as Silents skillfully constructed procedures to promote such values. By trying to anticipate every possibility, and by expecting good will from all sides to listen and make adjustments, Silent leaders have sought to serve the greater good.

Positively, this meant that more people in a group had a chance to influence decision-making. More African Americans, other minorities, and women were elected to Congress in the 1980s and 1990s (years of Silent generation domination) than ever before.[11] Creativity blossomed as differing views were aired. Negatively, this Adaptive-style leadership is prone to a mania for minutiae and for intricate procedures, processes, and precedents. (Adaptives tend to make great bureaucrats.) Eighty-four congressional committees had oversight responsibility for the Department of Housing and Urban Development just prior to the multibillion-dollar savings-and-loan scandal, and still a scandal happened.[12]

Strauss and Howe say a great deal more about Adaptive generations in leadership across society and throughout history. Let us look at religious leadership as an Adaptive generational type has moved through midlife.

Religious Leadership, Silent Style

As the Silent generation entered midlife, they also moved into high office in the church. The elevation of Joseph Bernardin to bishop of Cincinnati and William Baum to archbishop of Washington, D.C., marked the arrival of this generation's leaders among Roman Catholics. Protestants saw church historian Martin E. Marty, magazine editor James M. Wall, and TV pastor Robert Schuller gain prominence and influence.

This is the generation whose members currently hold power within their faith communities or are just passing leadership (in many cases) to the coming Boomers. What do Silents believe and stress in the faith? What is the shape of their leadership? How do they communicate from pulpit and word processor? Where do they put their time, talent, and treasure in church?

If asked to fill in the blank, "God is _____," Adaptive generations choose the word "love." This generational type tries to embody the image of God as a warm, gentle, welcoming parent. Adaptives' faith echoes Paul's letter to the Corinthians as they too believe "love is patient and kind . . . believes all things, hopes all things and endures all things" [1 Cor. 13:4, 7]. Theirs is a touching faith that, given enough chances, a sinner can be reformed. For Adaptive generations, love is expressed as forgiveness, acceptance, tolerance, and a nonjudgmental attitude. (At times their acceptance is seen as so elastic that others accuse them of standing for nothing, and therefore falling for anything.)

Adaptives often show a high degree of patience, and a knack for finding an alternative when others are locked into an either/or stance. As Enlightener Nathaniel Appleton, a pastor, wrote in 1743, "[T]he function of a minister is pointing out those middle and peaceable ways, wherein the truth generally lies, and guarding against extremes on the right hand and on the left."[13] Compromiser William Channing believed that Trinitarianism was a prime source of trouble and strife among Christians. He offered Unitarianism as a middle way among competing denominations, becoming the first president of the American Unitarian Association in 1825.

Especially in the work of its pioneer feminists, the Silent generation reconsidered male theological assumptions. Through a great deal of fresh textual work with Scripture, Phyllis Trible, Rosemary Radford Ruether, and others enriched theological thinking with feminine imagery for God and gender-inclusive language. Indeed, they stressed that God is beyond definition and that human language is inadequate for describing God. On the other hand, since human language and imagery are the tools we have for describing the indescribable, these theologians argued that we should press our language and thinking to their limits and use as rich a palette as possible. At least we should not *mislead* others, and at best perhaps all our inadequate pieces and descriptions of God and God's work might be more accurate.

Solomon serves Adaptive generations as a biblical model. In Solomon's time Israel had peace and prosperity, the Psalms and Proverbs were collected, and history to that time was recorded (Torah, 1 and 2 Samuel). Solomon built the Temple, dedicated it with style, opened trade routes, tolerated the alternative beliefs of his wives and concubines, and found flexible ways to exact taxes. Solomon assuaged tribal tensions and managed to postpone an eruption of worship wars (Jerusalem vs. Bethel) until after his death.

Positive Religious Leadership Traits

Adaptive church leaders seek to include everyone in the circle of God's love. They practice inclusivity, and genuinely appreciate the strengths of multiculturalism. Adaptives strive for consensus to weld the diversity articulated at the leadership table into a whole greater than the sum of its parts. They believe a good process will promote consensus. If the process is well designed, and takes into account all contingencies, then fairness can be embodied, and inclusiveness is the result. If decisions are kept provisional and can be appealed, then those on the losing side have a chance to both to heal and to bring new facts and arguments to bear that may have been overlooked or underweighted.

Positively, Silent leaders are inclusive, careful, detail oriented, empathetic, procedure minded, and precedent honoring. They listen well, make adjustments to formal rules to allow for human situations, and often invent ways for soft-spoken or previously ignored members and leaders to express themselves, whether in leading, developing and displaying talent, or exploring new personal possibilities. They make fine moderators, excellent reconcilers, and useful parliamentarians in heated assemblies. They often make excellent pastoral counselors by providing a sympathetic ear, using multiple therapeutic approaches, and deferring and referring to mental health experts in timely and appropriate ways.

Adaptives like the Silent generation stress acceptance and tolerance within Christianity, and beyond Christianity toward other faiths. Adaptives would be unlikely to lead a Crusade against infidels since they find it very hard to think of another belief system as just wrong. Their openness is seen in the American phrase "Well, at least they believe in *something*." Silent-controlled church bodies have sought to atone for past sins by issuing apologies to the Jews (the Evangelical Lutheran Church in America, for the anti-Semitism of Martin Luther) and to African Americans (the Southern Baptist Convention, for slavery.)

Other generations expect this open-minded tolerance from Adaptives, and are upset and dismayed when it is not expressed. For example, the Revs. Jerry Falwell and Pat Robertson attracted enormous attention and controversy in the 1980s as leaders of the Moral Majority and the Christian Coalition, respectively. Part of the reason for the frenzy surrounding their activities was generational. They are both members of an Adaptive generation, whom people expected to be warm, open, accepting, flexible, understanding, and at home with multiculturalism and diversity. But these two pastors' fundamentalist theological reasoning led them to be stern, delimiting, inflexible, and judgmental, and made them the (perhaps unwitting) spokesmen for a white Southern male power structure that felt threatened by social change.

Promoting inclusiveness and tolerance, Adaptive religious leaders at times are surprised that their efforts touch off controversy. When Lutherans and Episcopalians decided (finally!) to ordain women, a number of leaders were dismayed at the degree to which this decision upset some traditionalist members and leaders.

In 1992 some national and regional executives of the Presbyterians (PCUSA) and the United Methodists were involved in organizing and leading a feminist conference in Minneapolis. Many members and leaders in these churches were dismayed at both the turn to mysticism and the apparent departure from classic Christianity shown at the conference. The Silent generation's national leaders in these churches were shocked at the storm of protest and accusations of paganism that broke open in regional and national gatherings. They swung into action to try to repair the breach, but often found parishioners and congregations leaving and contributions curtailed or redirected.

Negative Religious Leadership Traits

As to the corresponding weaknesses in the Silent leadership approach, other generations are not shy about noting these. (In many cases the Silents themselves would be the first to identify and own up to their own weaknesses.) Many Adaptive leaders have such faith in consensus as a goal that they may find it hard to admit that consensus is not possible on some issues. They can be haunted by the thought: "If we just give this another hour [week, four more meetings], we'll get to a point at which we all agree."

Adaptive church leaders' high value on forgiveness can lead them beyond the limits of what many consider historic orthodoxy. Compromiser Henry Ballou's 1805 *Treatise on the Atonement* denied that anyone would be punished in the afterlife and asserted that all would be saved by a loving and forgiving God—in short, Universalism. Ballou is honored as one of the founding theologians of this idea.[14]

The Silent generation's sense of fairness and inclusivity and its penchant for expanding choices for the previously marginalized have also led Silents to explore the ordination of openly homosexual ministers. The Universal Fellowship of Metropolitan Community Churches and the United Church of Christ have opened the door to such ordinations, upsetting many Christians, but giving hope to some in other denominations. Among Lutherans, Methodists, Episcopalians, and others, the Silents are also the generation that is seeking some means of affording church blessings for gay couples in committed relationships. Many Silents are genuinely hurt and puzzled that such actions have caused benevolence boycotts and fomented threats of schism.

Silent leaders can overlook how time-consuming relational issues and consensus-building can be. Their preference for inclusivity and process expands the number of seats needed on decision-making groups, stretches and multiplies meetings, and frustrates the more action-minded group members. A process built toward these ends becomes increasingly complex—there are more ifs, ands, and buts to consider from every point of view. (Silent leaders will ask in reply, "Isn't it worth it sometimes?") The process also grows longer. One Silent-dominated church council grew to 24 lay members, plus four clergy and several lay department heads. The once voiceless had a seat at the table, but such a large group had an intimidating effect on many at that table. Just giving each person the floor for a two-minute self-introduction used up the better part of an hour.

Excessive attention to detail and a lengthy process can give church members and fellow leaders the impression that these leaders are cautious to the point of timidity. Members of a governing group can be perceived as using process and procedure to avoid coming to decisions that may be unpopular in the eyes of some. Hence even Silents urge each other on with the cry, "Not to decide is to decide." Some Silents' desire to leave decisions open-ended and to honor multiple appeals denies everyone a sense of closure. Silents are vulnerable to endless revisiting of what others see as trivial points.

Having come through the agony of reaching a decision, Silents can be loath to change it. Sometimes they think those still opposed to the decision are uncaring. ("After all, we have had *all* these meetings, covered *all* this ground, taken *so much* into account, made all the adjustments, and you weren't there for all that.") Opponents (particularly those from other generations) are dismayed to find rigidity where they expect flexibility, and are miffed by the implication that they are ignorant.

Communication

Through all the twists and turns of the times the Silent generation's leaders have continued their earnest and diplomatic approach to church issues and conflicts. As they convey their understanding of their faith, Silents usually come well equipped with strong formal education credentials, much life experience, and often a raft of continuing-education credits. They are also a generation with many skilled communicators.

Their religious values and emphases come through in their vocabulary choices. Their speech and writing may be studded with terms like multiculturalism, inclusiveness, inclusivity, openness, flexibility, acceptance, and diversity. Their communication is often polysyllabic, since many Silents are keen on finding a word or phrase that will convey exactly the right shade of meaning or level of nuance.

This talent and precision with words has made Silents a formidable theological generation. The gifted among them have produced works of lasting impact, as seen in this table. Pastors and church leaders will recognize the careful and thorough character of many of these works, and know their impact in Bible colleges and seminaries.

TABLE OF SILENT GENERATION RELIGIOUS CONTRIBUTORS

Birth year	Name	Background and contribution
1926	J. I. Packer	Anglican theologian and pro-inerrantist; *Knowing God* (1973) and *I Want to Be a Christian* (1979).
1926	Lyle Schaller	Methodist researcher; member of Yokefellow Institute; prolific writer of over 80 books on congregational dynamics and pastoral issues.
1927	John Yoder	Mennonite leader and writer; *The Politics of Jesus* (1972), *Body Politices* (1992).
1928	Donald Bloesch	Evangelical theologian; *Essentials of Evangelical Theology* (2 vols.,1978 and 1998), *Jesus Christ: Lord and Savior* (1997).

1928	Raymond E. Brown	Roman Catholic theologian and writer; *The Gospel of John* (Anchor Bible, 1969), *The Birth of the Messiah* (1976), *Giants of the Faith* (1998).
1928	Andrew Greeley	Moderate-liberal Roman Catholic priest, researcher, popular author, columnist; *The Making of the Popes* (1979), *The Cardinal Sins* (1981), *The Catholic Imagination* (2000).
1928	Martin E. Marty	Lutheran scholar, columnist, and author; an editor since 1950s of *The Christian Century; Righteous Empire* (1986), *Education, Religion, and the Common Good* (2000).
1929	Martin Luther King	African American Baptist minister and civil rights activist; Nobel Peace Prize (1964).
1929	William Pannell	African American educator; *My Friend, the Enemy* (1968), *Evangelism from the Bottom Up* (1992).
1929	Ruth Carter Stapleton	Spiritual healer; sister of President Jimmy Carter; *The Gift of Inner Healing* (1976).
1930	Beverly LaHaye	Founder and president, Concerned Women for America; *The Spirit Controlled Woman* (1976).
1930	Hal Lindsey	Author and evangelical pastor; *The Late, Great Planet Earth* (1970), *The Final Battle* (1995).
1930	Pat Robertson	Baptist pastor and broadcaster; founder, Christian Broadcast Network (1959), and "The 700 Club" (1968).
1931	Charles Colson	Nixon presidential assistant; founder of prison ministry network, author: *Born Again* (1976), *Loving God* (1983).
1931	Harvey Cox	Baptist-trained theologian and later defender of liberal Protestantism; *The Secular City* (1988), *Fire from Heaven* (1994).
1933	Jerry Falwell	Baptist pastor and political activist; founder, Moral Majority; *Listen America* (1984).

1934	John Dominic Crossan	Roman Catholic theologian and writer; *The Historical Jesus* (1993), *Jesus and Faith* (1994).
1934	Charles Swindoll	President, Dallas Theological Seminary; *Improving Your Serve* (1984), *The Mystery of God's Will* (1999).
1936	James Dobson	Colorado psychologist; founder, Focus on the Family; *The Strong-Willed Child* (1985), *Bringing Up Boys* (2001).
1936	Richard J. Neuhaus	Former Lutheran cleric, professor, and writer; became a Roman Catholic priest, *The Naked Public Square* (1984), *Doing Well and Doing Good* (1992), editor, *First Things*.
1936	Rosemary Ruether	Roman Catholic feminist theologian and author; *Sexism and God-Talk* (1983), *Contemporary Catholicism: Crisis and Challenges* (1987).
1938	James Cone	African American theologian and advocate of liberation theology; *Black Theology* (1993).
1939	Ron Sider	Educator and ethicist; *Rich Christians in an Age of Hunger* (1973), *Just Generosity* (2000).
1939	David Tracy	Roman Catholic theologian and writer; *Blessed Rage for Order* (1975).
1941	Jesse Jackson	Baptist minister; political activist; founder of Rainbow Coalition and PUSH (People United to Save Humanity).

From both pulpit and pen, this highly credentialed generation can communicate with intimacy, warmth, knowledge, and understanding. Many Silents can say with genuine sincerity, "The essence of humanity is feelings." Their insight into human emotions and strong ability to focus on each individual can make their words touching and powerful without becoming maudlin. As such, they often make beloved pastors and preachers with their care-filled and intimate illustrations. For instance, I think they might explain part of the Parable of the Good Samaritan like this:

The Samaritan's compassion was strong enough to overcome his biases. The earliest piece of Christian sculpture in existence, dating from the second century, depicts the Good Samaritan tenderly and gently lifting the victim onto his donkey. Jesus uses this parable to illustrate how divine love works in human beings. Such love causes the Samaritan to give of himself, of his supplies, of his time, and of his courage. The divine love flows so strongly in this Samaritan that he even agrees to be a source of third-party, private-sector medical reimbursement.

Their liabilities as communicators here parallel those seen in leadership. Silents can be prone to getting lost in the charm and detail of their own stories. The temptation to digression is strong. One heart-warming insight can trigger another and another. At times, parishioners can be more overwhelmed than charmed, inspired, or informed. Silent generation communicators can find it a challenge to say "what it all means" in one crisp line. (This is the generation that convenes a committee to write a four-page, single-spaced mission statement.) The generation's tendency and expectation, often reinforced by a strong academic background, is to qualify, modify, and footnote endlessly. In this Silents resemble their 1980s peer from the TV series "Star Trek: Next Generation," Captain Jean-Luc Picard. He could stand on the ship's bridge and intone in 14 syllables, "Activate the starboard lateral sensor array." (A Generation X commander would probably simply snap out in four syllables, "Right sensors on!")

Stewardship

Beyond general leadership tasks like communication, how do generational insights affect parish issues? While many possible areas could be pondered (adult education, worship, outreach, pulpit search committees, to name a few) let's take a look at a recurring challenge for religious leaders— stewardship. How can leaders apply generational understandings to use the gifts of time, talent, and treasure that God has given to the members of a congregation? We will look at this area for each of the four generational types, for here one size does not fit all.

In 2002, the youngest of the Silent generation were turning 60; the eldest, 77. A generation's traits and its members' place in the life cycle color giving patterns and expectations of stewardship. The upper end of this generation is generally comfortably retired. These people's income is usually a combination of Social Security; payments from some of the last, old-style defined-benefit corporate pensions; payouts from newer IRA, Keogh and 401(k) plans; and a nest egg from cashing out their home equity. Younger members are at their peak earning years as they hold the reins in numerous businesses, organizations, and governmental bodies. Education expenses for children and often mortgage payments are behind them and their discretionary income is at its maximum.

There are claims on these income sources. Many of this often-divorced generation make alimony payments. Many others are providing income support, down payments and/or house payments for their strapped Generation X children and stepchildren. A fraction of Silents are even raising their grandchildren and step-grandchildren in their condos and townhouses (or dismal apartments in high-rise ghettos), bearing a second round of child-rearing expenses.

When church leaders plan stewardship efforts, they can keep several themes in view that will bring a stronger response from the Silent generation.

Relationships. Members of this warm-hearted and friendly generation especially value human relationships and friendships, so they are glum if approached only once a year for money. The time to begin the annual stewardship drive is at the close of last year's drive by establishing and building such relationships. Calling at home, making shoot-the-breeze phone calls, dropping an occasional note in the mail, or sending a day-brightener e-mail to pass along are all good. A "have a safe trip" and a "welcome back" card sent to this Frostbelt-Sunbelt generation of church snowbirds will be well received. Birthday and anniversary greetings are good *if* they are personal—a monthly printed list in the newsletter or worship bulletin is not enough. When appropriate, a somewhat-longer-than-average hospital visit, with an "I've got all the time in the world" air, will be much appreciated.

Surprisingly, such relationship building seems to work best when the leader (not necessarily the pastor; a committed lay leader is often even more successful) is not a fellow Silent. Surveys of this generation have shown that a majority of members wish they were of some other age or generation. Inwardly they lament that they were born 10 years too soon or five years too late. Through members of other generations they can vicariously scratch this itch.

Adaptive generations more than others are alert to the complexities and interconnections of life. Pastors can plow the ground for an annual drive by making stewardship references year around and linking them to the fabric of church life. A two-week sermon series with a stewardship emphasis in late February and a three-week one in early June set the table nicely for a November campaign.

This generation likes creating and expanding choices and opportunities, especially for the previously marginalized in church and society. Starting a Habitat for Humanity group, or having the church join and support the InterFaith Hospitality Network for temporarily homeless families, or helping a battered women's shelter get off the ground will have appeal.

Adaptives generally want the church to embody the humanity of Jesus and the love of God. Start-up funding to establish a pastoral-counseling post in a large church, or day-care tuition scholarships for single mothers, or installation of new, individual sound systems for the hearing-impaired in the worship space are good examples of such caring.

Adaptive generations have a pattern of supporting artists, underwriting local theaters, opera companies, orchestras, and museums. If a congregation is going to repaint its building, refurbish the pipe organ, install or refinish stained-glass windows, or purchase a set of conga drums for a new contemporary worship service, this is the generation to ask. If the worship space needs a new piano, a Silent couple may well buy it, and not even want a memorial plaque mounted. Their modesty can be engaging—if a bit mystifying to more forward generations.

Strategies. Leaders should publicize goals well in advance of the actual time of asking for contributions. If they can build in some flexibility by either adding or dropping a goal or two on the way to the actual appeal, so much the better in the eyes of the Silents.

Leaders should provide written explanations for given goals. A detailed rationale that can be passed out will convince this generation that its leaders have done their homework. Financial information in such a pamphlet can be noted to the penny, showing a welcome attention to detail. (If a new piano will cost $7,481.16, tax, delivery, and set-up included, say so. No need to round up to $7,500.)

Finally, this heavily credentialed generation respects experts in various fields. Silents will enthusiastically support bringing in an outside stewardship consultant or capital-funds advisor, because such a person can provide real expertise. Alternatively, if the stewardship team can attend a conference featuring such an expert, this will be seen as a great positive. Leaders can note such experts in their pre-drive publicity and materials.

The Stewardship Request

When asking for a commitment to the annual campaign or a capital funds drive from members of the Silent generation, church leaders can make several points:

- Silents often like face-to-face, relational meetings. Many of them would like to meet you somewhere for lunch. Don't be surprised if your congregant offers to pick up the check.
- Be prepared to listen at length. There may be a long conversation that either (a) finally meanders around to a long talk about the financial issue at hand, or (b) deals with the money matter casually, almost in passing.
- Use personalized, intimate stories to make your appeal. "Do you know Mrs. Barton, who sits up on the pulpit side, fourth pew from the front? Last Sunday she came up to me after worship just delighted about how well she could hear, thanks to the new personal sound system."
- As a leader you should know the budget in detail. Your precision indicates you have done your homework.
- In asking for a pledge this year, stress the aspect of a fair share and proportionate giving—you have been blessed to be a blessing. You might say, "Two families have put in $_____ for the _____ , and they can afford it. We also have $_____ from a family who really can't afford it, what with their heating bills being so high. I'd like to ask you for a pledge of $_____ as your fair share to this effort."
- Be bold in asking for a contribution. Silents often have the discretionary income to make a sizable gift. Even if Silents can't make a large gift, they are flattered to be asked. The Rev. Walt Kallestad, a large-church pastor, shared this account in a 1995 talk: When the Rev. Robert Schuller, a pastor of the Reformed Church of America, set about building the Crystal Cathedral in the early 1970s, he struck up a relationship with a Lutheran businessman at a Rotary Club lunch. Schuller later visited this active layman at his office to ask him for a contribution to the church construction project. When the businessman pulled out his personal checkbook, he asked Schuller, "Do you have a figure in mind?" Schuller glanced around the executive's grand office and said, "Yes. I think you are in a position to contribute $1 million." There was a long pause, and then the businessman said, "I believe you're right" and wrote out the check.

- When appropriate—when a Silent member has financial savvy—invite him or her to help the congregation establish an endowment fund, create a foundation, expand a memorial fund, or begin a "wills awareness effort" to encourage members to leave bequests to the church.

Into Elderhood

While the youngest of this generation is turning 60, its oldest members are in their late 70s. These frequent-flyer elders are changing the face of retirement in the U.S. Some still relocate to Sunbelt retirement communities. When they find condo association rules excluding people under a certain age, they work for change and repeal. Many more are staying in their own communities, selling off suburban split-levels and moving into urban townhouses and condos. In both cases home serves as a base for travel, some of it exotic: Antarctic penguin feeding cruises, exploring the ruins of Cambodia's Angkor Wat, or Jordanian archeological digs.

Silents are also reforming geriatric health care. These are the patients who visit doctors armed with information about drug descriptions, possible diagnoses, and alternative treatments, all downloaded from the Internet. Their health-care reforms have turned traditional nursing homes into transitional-care facilities for patients released from hospitals but not yet ready for home. Their preferences for more options and more personal solutions have led the Centrum Silver generation to rewrite Medicare rules to include more home nursing, home therapy, and home hospice options.

As these latest Adaptives look back on their lives and ponder their legacy to future years, several patterns are emerging.

1. *In general, Adaptive generations are often economically comfortable deep into old age.* Silents have transformed their retirement income sources so that mostly they will not burden their families or society. They combed through the tax code to uncover section 401, paragraph (k), and section 403, paragraph (b), and publicized them to the business community. They added IRA, Keogh, S.I.M.P.L.E. and Roth-IRA to everyone's vocabulary. They also added portability provisions and shortened vesting periods to traditional pension plans.

This array of alternate senior income sources has allowed the Silent generation to change the tenor of national debates about Social Security and loosened the hold the AARP lobby has had on this subject. As the

Silents have replaced the GIs in influencing geriatric issues, they have multiplied choices and possibilities for future generations. Proposals such as means-testing Social Security benefits, raising the retirement age, and partial Social Security privatization are all circulating as ideas and plans because the Silent generation is not as defensive as the GIs about public spending on the elderly.

2. *This relative prosperity has given Silents the means for repairing some of the damage their early marriages and rising divorce rate caused their children.* They can welcome home their Generation X children who have taken a pummeling in the dot-com economy. These Adaptives also quietly provide income supplements to their grown children, and come through with the down payment for starter or move-up houses. They frequently underwrite business start-ups, function as venture capitalists, and serve as financial angels and senior advisors behind all sorts of small, struggling, but promising firms.

Members of this generation are also bonding with their grandchildren and step-grandchildren through some of the things that money can buy. The travel industry notes a strong trend toward "grand-travel"—grandparents taking grandchildren on trips (while "seniors-only" group travel is showing a decline).[15] A new Adaptive generation will start to be born around 2005 and the Silent bond with these new Adaptives will lead to more gentle involvement in the lives of these youngsters.

3. *When the aging Silents turn their gaze beyond their families toward church and country, they will continue to make their quiet, polite, and earnest mark.* In congregations the Silents are the greeters and Sunday afternoon callers who meet the visitors from that morning. They are the ushers who make everyone feel welcome in the pews. They can be invited to visit Sunday-school rooms as surrogate grandparents and storytellers of the faith.

For church and synagogue, Silents form a wonderfully gifted cadre of retired visitation pastors and rabbis. Their generational gifts in human relationships make them eagerly awaited visitors in the assisted-living facility, the nursing home, the hospital, or at home.

Their generational assets also make clergy of this generation able interim clergy. Their flexibility and diplomacy, combined with their innate warm-heartedness, enable them to help congregations grieve the end of one ministry, focus on new possibilities and options, develop a process that includes a broad range of voices for input, and pave the way for a new leader.

In the larger society Silents will continue to embody both civility and flexibility in accepting human limitations and failings. As long as they demonstrate this nimble-footedness, younger generations will admire and learn from these well-mannered seniors. Historically, elders of Adaptive generations have insisted on personal modesty, fairness, and the offering of human hope to the downtrodden. Compromiser John Quincy Adams, after serving as U.S. president, went back to Massachusetts and became the only president ever subsequently elected to Congress. When the Africans on board the slave-trade ship *Amistad* revolted, killed the crew, and attempted to sail back to Africa, they shipwrecked in New England and were imprisoned. Adams took their appeal to the Supreme Court (which had several slave-holding justices serving at the time) and won their freedom and repatriation to Africa.[16]

Finally, as death claims increasing numbers of the Silent generation, they will show younger generations that death need not be a fearsome thing. Rather, death is a transition from limited to unlimited possibilities and into the presence of Love.

They will often prefer to die at home, among family and friends. Silents will plan more often for a memorial service than a traditional funeral. Such memorials will occur much further past the death date than a typical funeral of the past as cremations become steadily more common. They will be a celebration of the life of the deceased as much as occasions for mourning. Poster boards with favorite photos will evolve toward VHS, CD-ROM (and soon DVD) multimedia presentations playing continuously during a memorial meal. There will be prerecorded farewell messages from the deceased and favorite music.

As Silents' estates enter probate, look for surprises embedded in their wills. Silents will use their bequests to endow churches, the performing arts, and foundations that support the disadvantaged. Such institutions will be astounded at the size of some of these bequests, because they will come from people who lived a very modest lifestyle. Expect occasional public court fights, as heirs battle to limit these bequests to leave a larger amount for the relatives.

These then are the Adaptives, earnest generations making a quiet and humane contribution to life in the church. They focus on the human dimension of the faith, in its frailties and possibilities. They understand better than other generations human limitations and the power of forgiveness and welcome, and these make a tender and cherished legacy.

CHAPTER 6

THE CLASH OF IDEALS

We turn to William Strauss and Neil Howe's work in *Generations* to trace another type through the stages of life. These authors identify the Idealist type appearing in American history with the following birth years and designations:

IDEALIST GENERATIONS	
Birth Years	**Name** **used by Strauss & Howe**
1942-1960	Boom
1860-1882	Missionary
1792-1821	Transcendentalist
1700-1723	Awakener
1584-1614	Puritan

Youth

Certain periods in America history have been fraught with danger, doubt, suffering, and sacrifice. During such times national (or, in the 1860s, sectional) unity is high; goals are clear. (Awakeners: "These colonies of a right ought to be free and independent!") As the end of a national crisis glimmers just ahead, people of all ages begin to realize, "Just a little longer and we'll be done!" An abrupt release of the strain comes as Cornwallis surrenders at Yorktown, Lee meets Grant at Appomattox, or the *USS Missouri* sails into Tokyo Bay.

The nation turns its productive energies from war production to making peace. The newly discharged soldiers and sailors apply their expertise to producing civilian goods for themselves and their neighbors. Births burgeon as returning war veterans marry the girls they left behind, while members of the younger, stay-behind generation, eager to prove their adulthood, marry early. Babies are born into a time of great construction of vast private and public works.

Life is generally good for kids born into such an era. The grown-up world is safe, settled, and prosperous. The economy hums, and the middle class expands. When Idealist generations are born, the latest medical arts for childbirth are applied. In the early 1800s doctors in large numbers began replacing traditional midwives and delivering Transcendentalist babies with forceps.[1] In the 1950s, the most modern medical birth techniques called for the pregnant woman to go to a hospital, receive a general anesthetic and give birth while unconscious, fully taken care of by the medical establishment. Her husband waited in the fathers' waiting room until a uniformed nurse brought a newborn Boomer into view behind a glass window that sealed off the medical equipment from unscientific, suspect laymen. The infant was bottle-fed, while drugs were administered to the mother to keep her body from producing breast milk.

A generation born into such an era finds adults busy, bustling, and building. Institutions of government, business, religion, and labor are strong, commanding loyalty and even earning a measure of affection for the prosperity they provide. With the outside world peaceful and prosperous, children are encouraged to explore their inner selves and to express preferences and individuality. In the early 1800s parents (especially mothers) of these prized infants began calling them by name, rather than "it" or "Baby."[2] Better infant survival rates meant that parents could risk greater emotional investment in their children. Broad prosperity meant that parents had increasing means to provide for children, such as child-size furniture. In 1863 Thomas Nast popularized a bearded, benign Santa Claus who brought Christmas gifts to deserving children.[3] In the postwar 1940s Gerber struggled to keep up with the demand for its baby food, high chairs, and plastic-headed, steel diaper pins. In the 1950s fortunes were made by the makers of Lionel trains, hula hoops, coonskin caps, Erector sets, and Schwinn and Huffy bikes.

Such eras see a sharp, gender-based division of labor, with women ruling the home and raising the children. (In particular the Civil War-era Missionary generation was proportionately the most fatherless of any American generation. According to historian Shelby Foote, losses of men of military and child-rearing age in some Southern states numbered as high as one in four.[4]) Mothers love their children with large doses of unconditional love. In religious terms, children from early on experience a life of grace; forgiveness is frequent. The downside of all this acceptance and forgiveness to the point of indulgence is cheap grace. Children conclude—with little evidence to the contrary—that sins against God or other human beings have no *real* consequences.

Men work in regimented, orderly, hierarchical institutions, providing outside-the-home brain and brawn for the larger economy. At home they increasingly take on the role of rule-enforcer ("Wait until your father gets home!") This gender division between omnipresent, hardworking, ever-caring mother, and rule-making, discipline-wielding and goods-providing father works an unusual effect on their children's view of God. Children see unconditional love, grace, acceptance, and support presented in a female package, while absence, judgment, punishment, and the power to produce are tied to males. Transferred to images and expectations of God, Idealist generations tend to link pleasurable and positive traits of God to the feminine. The more difficult, distant, and painful attributes of God are linked to the masculine.

Children form these links internally behind a flurry of outward religious activity. Kids are taken to brand-new religious buildings, often featuring longer pews to accommodate larger family sizes; and families are expected to sit together. Youth are allowed few if any excuses for skipping worship services.

When Idealists are children, congregational adults emphasize living in the community, fitting in, and getting along, using the image of the family of God. Children in such congregations find traditions carefully observed and handed down. Religion takes on the character of a series of duties and a list of good works. Busy, teamwork-oriented adults are prone to equate depth of faith with the number of good works.

Sunday school and religious education are also a given. In such periods teachers and youth pastors tend to be left-brained and rationalistic. What such teachers convey are the stories and facts of the faith. This approach can lead to a "head trip" orthodoxy. That is, each denomination imparts a certain body of knowledge about the path to salvation. Adults teach traditional catechetical formulas and celebrate memorized, traditional responses from youth. (Lutheran leaders ask, "What does this mean?" and Lutheran confirmands are to reply, "We are to fear and love God so that . . ." Baptist leaders implore, "Accept Jesus as your *personal* Lord and Savior"; they hope Baptist youth will answer "Praise the Lord! Jesus is in my heart.")

Children in such times, encouraged by their parents to be introspective and individualistic, can often sense a hollowness in all this faith activity. Traits learned from their mothers lead these generations to seek inner meaning and ever-richer private experiences. A tension builds in Idealist generations as they watch their fathers conduct these public religious activities. Combined with the Idealists' ambiguity toward their fathers, the tension snaps as this generation comes of age in rising adulthood.

Therefore it is not surprising that teenage and young-adult rebellion will focus on avoiding or overcoming a masculine, powerful, angry God. Young adults from such generations have a history of going off with like-minded peers in small groups, where love, acceptance, and even indulgence from other group members can echo what they picked up from their mothers.

Rising Adulthood

Members of Idealist generations come into adulthood looking for meaning and seeking an external world as rich as their inner lives. Mere economic activity and what appears as religious formalism repels them. For them the adult world of busy-bee fathers looks depressingly prosaic, artificial, and mechanical. Their highly individualistic explorations clash sharply with tangible realities, and an eruption ensues.

Their discontent boils over in a series of massive, youth-fired demonstrations and riots. As the Boomer generation of Idealists entered their 20s, many readers will remember the long, hot summers of the 1960s, filled with campus protests about Vietnam and the draft, and inner-city riots about racial discrimination.

Earlier Idealists have displayed this same noisy pattern upon entering adulthood. The Chicago Haymarket riot of 1886 marked the beginning of the Missionary generation's entry into adulthood. In an earlier era of campus unrest and disrespect for authority, Strauss and Howe report two-thirds of the Transcendentalist 1823 senior class at Harvard was expelled six weeks before graduation.[5] Indeed, the arrival of the Puritan generation at Plymouth Colony was the outcome of a similar revolt by college-educated youth against their high-liturgical fathers, members of the same generational cohort as King James I.

These generations throughout American history have touched off spiritual renewals and explorations, revivals and awakenings. The 1960s and 1970s saw the Boomers investigating Eastern mysticism and exploring alternate inner realities by using marijuana and Native American peyote and reading the books of Carlos Casteñada. Self-proclaimed Jesus People fervently entered (or renewed) a commitment to evangelical Christianity. Hal Lindsey and C. C. Carlson's *The Late, Great Planet Earth*, with its themes of rapture, apocalypse, and judgment upon a world gone bad, caught the fancy of Boomer readers looking for religious or spiritual underpinnings for their condemnation of a soulless, immoral society. A wave of peace-and-love communes sprang up in warehouse lofts, campus row houses and isolated farms, featuring supposed mutual harmony, chemical and sexual experimentation, common property ownership, and typically, a brief life span as a community.

The '60s consciousness revolution shows a strong resemblance to earlier Idealist generations at this life stage. This one was unusual in its spiritual exploration beyond the bounds of Christianity, but in other respects it was a familiar turn in the generational cycle.

As the turn-of-the-20th century Missionary generation hit this stage in life, Agnes Ozman spoke in tongues at Bethel Bible College of Topeka,[6] touching off an interest in gifts of the spirit. This Holiness movement culminated in the Azusa Street outpouring in Los Angeles in 1906 and the formation of the Assemblies of God denomination by Eudorus Bell in 1914.[7] The denomination commonly included whites and blacks together at a time when other churches practiced racial segregation in worship and membership. Other denominations that emphasized the inner, spiritual life made a place for women in the pulpit: the Pentecostal Holiness Church in 1895, and the Church of the Nazarene in 1908. The African Methodist Episcopal Zion Church amended its rules in 1898 to allow for the ordination of women. In 1904 Evangeline Booth (daughter of founder William Booth) became commander of the Salvation Army.[8]

Missionary Idealists also established communes, looked for an apocalypse, and excoriated the establishment. Congregational minister George Herron began a community in Georgia in 1896 that experimented with communal living arrangements. (It closed in 1900.[9]) The Jehovah's Witnesses looked with anxious anticipation for the in-breaking of the Kingdom of God and the appearance of heaven on earth in 1914 (the outbreak of World War I that year did undercut some of the enthusiasm.)

Walter Rauschenbush published his forceful critique of society, *Christianity and the Social Crisis*, in 1907.

Some Missionary voices were directed at other religious groups. Loud debates echoed through Protestant churches about "the Catholic problem" (brought on by a large migration from Southern and Eastern Europe), and "the Jewish issue" (fueled by a large migration from Russia). Some fervently advocated tolerance, looking for religious commonalities among these communities. Evangelical hard-liners reacted differently in 1905 by publishing a series of pamphlets called "The Fundamentals." They hoped to unite true Christians on the fundamentals of the faith in face of the threat posed by these non-Protestant bodies.

In yet an earlier turn of the generational cycle an Idealist generation (the Transcendentalists) shook America in the 1820s to the early 1840s. Tearful conversions and packed public meetings swept from Eastern city congregations to the western frontier post of Fort Dearborn and its little village of Chicago. Pressure for religious reform, hunger for spiritual experiences, and an interest in apocalyptic fervor rolled through religious groups. A Jewish Reform Society was formed in Charleston in 1825.[10] The Lutheran pietist followers of Hans Nielsen Hauge formed themselves into a denomination in 1846.[11] (Formal ordination was frowned upon, while the Haugeans celebrated the practice of speaking as prompted by the spirit of God, Quaker-style, by anyone during worship.) The Millerites (later the Seventh-day Adventists) published scores of magazines and books awaiting the end of the world in 1844.[12]

Efforts to achieve greater equality of women took shape. New York and Boston opened their first public high schools for girls in 1826. Oberlin College in Ohio was founded in 1833 as the country's first co-educational university.[13] Mount Holyoke College was established in 1837 as the first all-women's college.[14]

Perfectionist societies and communal living arrangements appeared. Joseph Smith, succeeded by Brigham Young, began a communal society that migrated from New York, to Ohio, to Illinois, to Missouri, and finally to the distant Utah Territory. From 1825 to 1830 Frances Wright ran a community at Nashoba, Tennessee. She and her followers purchased slaves from the surrounding plantations and then paid them at the wage level at which whites were commonly paid, so they could work off their purchase price in the community until they were free. The community also practiced strict equality between the sexes.[15]

Similar parallels can be found in the First Great Awakening of the 1730s and 1740s led by Jonathan Edwards, George Whitefield, and John Wesley, and the initial migration of the Puritans to New England in the 1600s.

The Idealists' questing for spiritual experience continues through rising adulthood and into midlife. So Boomers in the 1970s touched off the Charismatic renewal among Roman Catholics and mainline Protestants. Boomer attendance made the Assemblies of God and other Pentecostal groups the fastest-growing U.S. denominations of the 1970s.[16]

Boomers who arrive in congregations as seekers are interested in learning, but constantly check what they are being taught against their own spiritual experiences. They also feel free to disagree and argue, to join a congregation on principle and to leave a congregation on principle—inner, self-validating principles. They are raising havoc with the Roman Catholic hierarchy over the church's refusal to ordain women. They have ignited worship wars in many congregations, and have initiated contemporary worship using loose-leaf hymnals and screen-projected praise choruses.

Life Changes

The search for meaning extends into the workplace, where Idealists generally find disappointment. Some enter yeshivas, Bible colleges, and seminaries, where they can pursue their spiritual quests in a scholastic way. Others try out communal living arrangements or even cultic communities where they can seek a more mystical approach.

But the great majority enter the workforce. In entry-level jobs, the usual expectations are duty, doing things by the book, and gaining experience through repetition. None of this strikes Idealists as meaningful, and they prove to be workers whom employers find flighty or unstable. Reluctant to take orders lest they become like their order-taking fathers, they often take a sullen, pragmatic approach to their work, while seeking meaning and enrichment off the job. Recessions and stagflation (as in the 1970s), or bank panics (like those in 1893 or 1837) are typical. Not until they enter midlife do Idealists change their view of work.

All this personal exploration takes time, so Idealists are slow to make commitments, both private and public. As a generation, Boomers married later than any other generation since the early 20th century Missionaries.

(The Missionaries produced the highest percentage of women who never married among the generations for which records are available.[17]) Boomers often delayed having children until they had explored commitment and marriage. It was only as the eldest female members of the Boomer cohort heard their biological clocks loudly ticking at age 40 (in 1983) that Boomer childbearing began in earnest as an echo of their own birth numbers.

In 1983 an explosion of "Baby On Board" black-and-yellow placards could be seen bobbing in the windows of minivans (which first appeared in the 1984 model year) as Boomers began to set a new tone for parenting. Hospitals remodeled green-tiled, garishly lit delivery rooms into wood-paneled, lace-curtained, cotton-sheeted, more subtly lighted birthing centers. These were outfitted with ultrasound machines and fetal monitors. Some centers offered the option of underwater births. Nurse-midwives reappeared as part of the medical team. Fathers learned birth coaching in Lamaze natural childbirth classes. Unlike their GI generation mothers, who had been unconscious when they gave birth, Boomer mothers used epidural spinal blocks, which allowed them to greet their newborns with tears of joy and immediate breast-feeding.

After the baby came home in a state-mandated, rear-facing infant carrier, the mother supplemented breast milk with soy-based, preservative-free formula that moved from health-food stores onto mainstream grocery shelves. The couple debated with other Boomer parents over which was the more environmentally sound diaper choice—biodegradable disposable diapers, or 100 percent cotton with Velcro closures, washed and delivered weekly from a "green" laundry. Barney the Dinosaur and his team-playing friends elbowed their way to prominence alongside the older, urban-based "Sesame Street."

As children were enrolled in day care (having been put on the waiting list when the pregnancy was first detected by a home testing kit), Boomer parents eagerly awaited daily reports from the teachers of their two-year-olds. How are their motor skills developing? What about their spatial and pre-mathematical operations? Are they playing well with the other children while showing leadership traits? ("It's been over a month since Madison has needed a time out!") How is the class finger-painting project coming? Is the trip to the new children's museum this Friday or next? Boomer parents were determined to take an active interest in their children's lives to offset the neglect they perceived the Silents had shown toward Generation X.

Often the best day care Boomers found was at the local, big-box suburban megachurch. These new congregations not only featured high-quality day care for children, but they took a leaf from the Rev. Bill Hybels of the Chicago-area Willow Creek Community Church in other ways. They offered coffee, tea, cappuccino, bottled water and soft drinks between worship services. Those services often featured video clips or, in place of a traditional sermon, live interviews with spiritually aware individuals. A raft of small-group options aimed at these spiritual seekers also figured prominently.

Midlife

As Idealists enter midlife, their impact as leaders is felt across social institutions.

Children and schools

As Boomers become the dominant parenting generation in midlife, they continue to raise the bar for their celebrated Millennial children. Uniform test standards, while not enacted at the federal level, are being implemented in state after state. (Generation X parents are following the Boomer lead on this one.) Third-graders in Minnesota spend two full days with a number-two pencil making ovals on an answer sheet to measure their reading skills. The following week they do the same for their math skills. Debates swirl over whether suburban schools are excessively "teaching to the test." On the other hand, Boomer parents in distressed urban and rural districts are often agitating for school vouchers that will allow their children to attend well-equipped suburban schools.

Many veteran teachers are idealistic Boomers who endured the harsh years and difficult student bodies of Generation X, and who now are finely tempered practitioners of the art of teaching. Such teachers, along with principals and superintendents, are steadily raising the bar of standards for students. And not just for students: new and veteran teachers alike are facing their own batteries of state tests and toughening standards for renewal of teacher certification.

Workplace

In the labor force Idealists entering midlife begin to find significance and satisfaction in work, an important breakthrough for such a questing generation. Finding such meaning, they tend to want more of it, much more, so Boomers have abandoned their former suspicion of work. They now "live to work," 24 hours a day, seven days a week. Having risen to intermediate positions in corporations, they find that giving orders suits them much better than receiving them.

Moving into leadership positions, Idealists bring visionary, outside-the-box thinking and fresh ideas to their work. Not all these ideas pan out, and implementing the details of a good idea does not come easily to such a generation. Good ideas and breakthroughs are grandly rewarded, like a Henry Ford making a standardized Model-T auto steadily more affordable. Failed business ideas and their workers are left aside, like Pittsburgh steel workers in the 1980s or whaling fleet owners and crews in the 1850s.

Later in midlife and into elderhood an interesting alliance of types forms between Idealists and Nomads, who are the next-younger generation. The graying Idealists continue to provide vision and moral grounding (What should we be producing? How can we do that morally?). The coming Nomads sort through ideas and visions, test out what works and what doesn't, and provide realistic leadership to get an organization, a company, an army, or a nation to achieve the goal. Idealists like Benjamin Franklin and his Awakener peers, or Lincoln of the Transcendentalists, or Franklin Roosevelt of the Missionaries cast a national vision: independence, saving the Union, preserving freedom. The Idealists did not lead troops into battle, but handed the task to Nomad generation members like Washington, Grant, and Eisenhower.

Religious Leadership

Turning to life in the parish, what can we expect from the current crop of Idealists as they come to lead religious bodies? How will they lead? How will they change the focus of the faith? Boomers are (in 2002) just now assuming power in church, synagogue, mosque, and temple. Examples include religious researcher George Barna, Jr., megachurch pastor Hybels, and pastor Rick Warren, founder of Saddleback Ministries, who are establishing new paradigms for congregational life, growth, and discipleship. The recent elections of St. Paul Synod Bishop Mark Hanson as presiding bishop of the Evangelical Lutheran Church in America and of Judy Yudof, a laywoman, as president of the United Synagogue of Conservative Judaism signal the arrival of this generation at the very top of established religious bodies.

Looking back on prior Idealist generations gives us some clues of what to expect from Boomer religious leaders.

TABLE OF IDEALIST RELIGIOUS FIGURES

Years	Name	Contribution
1586–1659	Lady Deborah Moody	Anabaptist founder of Gravesend, Long Island, the only permanent settlement in colonial America planned and directed by a woman.
1591–1643	Anne Hutchinson	Massachusetts Puritan house church leader and rival to Governor John John Winthrop; found guilty of excessive spiritual enthusiasm. Exiled to Rhode Island.
1602(?)–1683	Roger Williams	Massachusetts Puritan exiled for denying right of state to interfere with religious beliefs. Founder of Rhode Island colony that practiced a religious freedom that welcomed Quakers, Jews, and atheists.
1703–1758	Jonathan Edwards	Congregationalist minister, leader of Great Awakening of 1730s and 1740s. Famed for sermon "Sinners in the Hands of an Angry God." Author, *Freedom of the Will* (1754): "We are free only when the Holy Spirit controls us."
1705–1787	Charles Chauncey	Congregationalist minister loudly opposed to Jonathan Edwards and the other New Lights. Leader of traditionalist Old Lights in face of revivals.

1706–1771	Shubal Stearns	Revivalist in North Carolina, founder (1755) of what became the Baptist denominations.
1713–1784	Junipero Serra	Wandering Franciscan who planted a chain of Catholic missions across Spanish colonial California.
1792–1875	Charles Finney	Professor, Presbyterian minister. Major figure in Second Great Awakening of 1820s to 1840s. Inventor of New Measures for conversion.
1797–1883	Sojourner Truth	Female slave freed in 1827. Wandered the Union following mystical voices and testifying to visions and advocating for abolition.
1793–1880	Lucretia Mott	Quaker preacher, abolitionist and women's rights activist.
1800–1831	Nat Turner	Free black Baptist minister who led a slave revolt in Virginia in 1831.
1801–1877	Brigham Young	Mormon leader of the Great Migration of the outcasts to the Utah territory in 1847. Successor to founder Joseph Smith.
1803–1882	Ralph Waldo Emerson	Congregationalist minister who developed Transcendentalism, which entailed a critique of excessive community complacency, materialism, and the pursuit of prosperity.
1805–1844	Joseph Smith	Founder of Mormonism, compiler of Mormon sacred texts in 1830s. Advocate of polygamy in a sectarian community.
1807–1871	Phoebe Palmer	Author of *The Promise of the Father*, vigorous defense of women's right to be ordained and to preach.

1817–1862	Henry David Thoreau	Leading Transcendentalist activist, communal leader. Author, *Civil Disobedience* (1849), *Walden* (1854).
1861–1918	Walter Rauschenbush	Author and social critic. *Christianity and the Social Crisis* (1907).
1862–1946	Alma Bridewell White	Founder and bishop of Pillar of Fire Church (1901). Publisher of magazine *Women's Chains*, which agitated for women's equality.
1863–1935	Billy Sunday	Early 20th century revivalist; one of the first to make extensive use of radio. Advocate of Prohibition.
1866–1923	Eudorus Bell	Ordained Baptist minister for 17 years. Converted to Pentecostalism. and founded Assemblies of God, 1914.
1881–1937	J. Gresham Machen	Conservative Biblical scholar, founder of Westminster Seminary, (1929) and founder and president of Orthodox Presbyterian Church, 1939. Author, *Origin of Paul's Religion* (1921) and *The Virgin Birth of Christ* (1930).
1943–	Cornel West	Controversial liberal African American professor of religion at Harvard, and then Princeton University. Author, *The American Evasion of Philosophy* (1989), *Keeping Faith* (1993), *Race Matters* (1993).
1945–	Luke Timothy Johnson	Catholic professor of New Testament; defender of Christian orthodoxy and ardent foe of Jesus Seminar, author, *The Real Jesus* (1996); *Living Jesus* (1999).
1945–	Judy Yudof	First woman chair of Council of Regional Presidents of the United Synagogue of Conservative Judaism.

1946–	William (Bill) McCartney	Founder of Promise Keepers, evangelical men's movement of 1990s stressing racial equality and male family responsibility.
1948–	Marva Dawn	Theologian, speaker, defender of traditional worship forms. Author, *Reaching Out without Dumbing Down* (1995), *A Royal Waste of Time* (1999), *The Unnecessary Pastor* (2000).
1948–	William (Bill) Hybels	Pioneer of megachurch parish model among Protestants. Early designer and advocate of contemporary worship forms to attract spiritual seekers (often fellow Boomers). Author, *Too Busy Not to Pray* (1988), *Becoming a Contagious Christian* (1994).
1950–	Thomas Bandy	Methodist church leadership consultant. Editor, *Net Results Journal.* Author, *Growing Spiritual Redwoods* (1997), *Kicking Habits* (1997).
1951–	Barbara Brown Taylor	Episcopal priest, educator, and renowned preacher. Author, *Bread of Angels* (1977), *Speaking of Sin* (2000).
1952–	Anthony (Tony) Campolo	Baptist sociologist, pastor; Founder, Evangelical Association for the Promotion of Education. Author of over 20 books; *Carpe Diem* (1994), *Revolution and Renewal* (2004).
1955–	Janet Marder	Rabbi, first woman to head Conservative Judaism National Rabbinic Association.
1955–	Martha Williamson	Television writer, executive producer, "Touched by an Angel," "Promised Land," religiously themed popular entertainment.

| 1957– | Michael Card | Influential contemporary Christian composer and singer. 22 albums. Author, *Parable of Joy* (1995), *A Violent Grace* (2000). |

In this list, one finds several common themes recurring among Idealist generations.

- Idealists seek spiritual experiences and loudly insist on freedom to pursue such experiences.
- Agitation for women's liberation and equality appears repeatedly in generations of this type.
- Arguments between Idealist generations and other generations, and arguments among Idealists themselves, are common.
- Idealist generations harshly criticize the existing social order and call for perfected human communities. In a generational cycle Idealists make attempts to establish such perfected communities.
- Idealist generations call for people and institutions to move away from things scientific, planned, artificial, and modern. Instead, Idealists celebrate and value that which is intuitive, spontaneous, natural, and folk-primitive.

Communications and Truth-telling

Idealists often communicate their visions in sweeping and compelling terms. Their language resounds with inspiration, calls for personal and social transformation, and praise for virtue and character. A Boomer preacher might expound on the import of the Good Samaritan something like this:

> Unlike the priest and the Levite who pass by the victim, the Good Samaritan's character expresses itself in compassion. Because of his inner values he is willing to break the rules of his day in order to do the right thing. The Spirit of God working through thim frees him from the prejudice between Samaritans and Jews.
>
> In that freedom he gives us a vision of how God works in the world. He sacrifices his time, his possessions, and his treasure to help. He even pledges to pay the innkeeper whatever it takes to put the victi back on his fee.

As congregational leaders, Idealists often embody George Bernard Shaw's famous words, "Some men see things that are and ask 'why?' Other men see things that never were, and ask 'why not?'" Such leaders see the promised land or, like John Winthrop, see a shining city on a hill.

In biblical terms Idealist generations bear a resemblance to Moses, who experienced several encounters with God beginning in Exodus 3. In his adulthood, Moses went to the seat of secular power (Pharaoh) to demand freedom, both physical ("Let my people go" [Exod. 5:1a]) and spiritual ("Let my people go so that they may hold a feast to Me in the wilderness" [Exod. 5:1]). Miriam appears alongside Moses in various leadership roles (for example, in Exod. 15:20). Moses argued with Aaron, quelled dissent (Massah and the water from the rock), and showed righteous anger toward those who worshiped a pagan god (the golden calf). Moses critiqued cosmopolitan life as the fleshpots of Egypt, and delivered commandments for an idealized society. Moses saw a future flowing with milk and honey and inspired those who followed him to believe in such a future for themselves.

Asked to fill in the blank in the statement "God is _____," members of Idealist generations will first modify the sentence to read "*My* God is ____." Their personal spiritual experiences come to the fore. In more extreme cases they want to make their view normative for other Idealists and other generational types. Of course other Idealists with different ideals also push to make *their* view normative. The upshot is that Idealists argue a lot, among themselves and with other generations.

They also argue because they complete the sentence as "My God is *Truth*." Their individual self-confidence, combined with a sense of the inherent rightness of their own view, leads them to be focused, no-compromise, passionate debaters. Their confidence in their personal understanding of faith also leads Idealists to be a splintery and divisive generation. Indeed, the 25,000 Puritans who covered New England with a string of settlements in a period of 15 years or so, from 1625 to 1640, did so in part because of this splintering tendency. Individual leaders who disagreed with each other, each one passionately self-assured, telling truth by their own perceptions (and theological hairsplitting), would draw off a group of like-minded followers to plant a new town[18] or even (in the case of Roger Williams in Rhode Island) a new colony.

The same passion for truth telling and vision lies behind Idealists' tendency to start new denominations or energize old ones. John and Charles

Wesley's and George Whitefield's initial efforts to plant Methodism in the 1730s, and Joseph Smith and Brigham Young's publication of new sacred writings to undergird the Mormons in the 1840s, are typical examples of new denominations. The post–Civil War wave of Scandinavian pietist immigrants filled Lutheran church bodies with new energy and social influence. The millions of Eastern European Jews who arrived after 1900 both refreshed American Reform Judaism, and established Conservative Judaism and Orthodoxy.

Stewardship

The leading edge of the Boomers (born 1943) stands on the brink of age 60, while the youngest members (born 1960) are in their early 40s, approaching midlife. If stewardship planners understand Boomer income and spending patterns, they can plan more effective stewardship campaigns.

- Many Boomers put off marriage and children, while many others did not, so that the ages of the Boomers' children cover a wide range. Some Boomers see their children earn master's degrees while others are just now hearing the cry of their firstborn in the delivery room. Consequently, Boomers face wildly differing educational costs for their children. Beyond public-school property taxes, Boomer parents pay everything from day-care fees to private academy tuition, from after-school lessons and traveling team expenses to postgraduate tuition.
- Both husband and wife are working. A wave of women pursuing careers alongside men has produced many two-income families. Scheduling stewardship events around two-career couples is often complicated. Work and home schedules can be difficult.
- As a rule Boomers are very hard working, having remade the American economy into its current 24/7 model. They often have either the income or the credit limits that allow them some rather conspicuous consumption (although they loathe the term). Boomer "starter castles" feature three-car garages filled with minivans, SUVs, and BMWs.
- Boomers feel extremely time-pressured by the 24/7 economy. Dual-income families in particular find time more precious than money. They have made Stephen Covey's *Seven Habits of Highly Effective People* a best seller, and have often attended life-management seminars that help them focus on what matters most in their lives so they can invest time in their priorities.

Stewardship Themes

Stewardship campaign planners may find the following ideas helpful in gaining a stronger response in time, talent and treasure from Boomers.

- The first theme is vision. Idealists are Joel-like generations, whose young people see visions, and whose old dream dreams. They want to see what their leaders see (even if they also want to disagree with it!), so a stewardship effort begins with a leader casting a vision before the people. The vision must be inspiring, delivered with passion and focused on the future. Making next year's budget does not qualify as a vision, nor does paying off some of the church mortgage (from 1982).
- If the vision is compelling enough, members of this generation can be asked to join the cause, although it may take time and argument to enlist Boomers. A helpful element of a campaign is a Q&A list about the vision, addressing anticipated objections. This information should also be posted on the congregational Web site. Idealists can be reluctant to make a commitment (marriage, children, career, church membership, political affiliation, etc.), so a long lead-time to allow for consideration and debate will help.
- Environmental concerns are a second theme that appeals to Boomers. For them, "being green" is not a leftover fad from the '70s. They really mean to make a difference in the natural world, whether through weekly recycling, or hand-demolishing condemned buildings so the structural components can be reused and the architectural detailings can be resold. A Sunday announcement that says "From now on, our congregation's coffee will come from a co-op that buys the beans directly from Guatemalan farmers who use organic growing methods" strikes Boomers as a double win for both the environment and for social justice.
- A third theme centers on children. Boomers highly value teaching virtue and building character in their children. So a proposed congregational day-care center can win Boomer support if presented along the lines of: "This day care will be a center that will value each child as special. We will staff it with teachers who model the spiritual values of this congregation so our children will have walking examples of the best in human beings. And by the way, we will build the playground out of recycled plastic, waste wood chips from a Native American tribal lumber mill, and surround the area with arsenic-free wood fencing."

The Stewardship Request

Asking members of the Boomer generation for their contribution to the stewardship effort of a congregation will go more smoothly when several factors are kept in mind.

- Despite some moves toward simplifying and downshifting, most Boomers still take a 24/7 approach to life, and often live to work. Many of them would be willing to meet over lunch near their place of work. Some will pick up the tab, while others will want to go Dutch.
- Calling on Boomers at home usually doesn't work well. They are as overscheduled at home as they are at work, and they often want home to be a refuge *from everyone and everything*—including the congregation.
- Whatever the setting, be prepared to listen at length, because Boomers usually want to talk. When it is the caller's turn to speak, Boomers will actually respect a stewardship visitor who expresses opinions opposed to their own.
- Callers should speak of congregational programs in terms of *upgrading* and *enhancing quality*, with a view toward making them *the best*: "We want to fund the new day-care director position so that we can get the best-qualified person, even if it is a strain on the budget and means a sacrifice for us."
- Callers should highlight parts of a budget or a capital funds campaign concerned with the environment, children, and social justice causes: "We want to take out six parking spaces at the lower end of the lot so our day-care kids can practice organic gardening."
- Callers can stress the spiritual benefits of being a member of a faith community that gives fuller meaning to life and work. Boomers who feel overworked and time-pressured respond positively to callers who can speak of the balance a spiritual dimension brings to one's life.
- Many Boomers are impressed to learn that summer religious camp experiences rank second only to the influence of their mothers in faith formation. Learning the significance of such camping moments opens up avenues for time and treasure contributions to support camps and youth ministry.

Elderhood Yet to Come

Americans are getting comfortable with the Silent generation in elderhood. These globetrotting, warm-hearted seniors continue to offer their families emotional and financial support, and fund new opportunities, artistic legacies, and counseling posts for congregations.

The Boomers in old age will be different. For now, of course, Boomers are mostly in denial about elderhood. To be sure, bursts of public concern are heard about Social Security, and many a Boomer gulps hard at each stock market hiccup reflected on his or her 401(k) quarterly statement. But mostly, Boomers are focused on their current stage of life; elderhood is still way out there. Fitness gyms are filled with sweating Boomers trying to stay firm and flexible. Laser eye surgery allows Boomers to correct their aging vision in a way that their parents couldn't. Retin-A and botox injections that mask facial age lines are in vogue. The beard or rubber-banded ponytail is shot through with gray until this week's application of Just 5 Minutes.

As the leading wave of former Idealist generations has passed 65 (about 2008 for the first Boomers), the country has usually entered a watershed crisis. In 1929 the oldest members of the Missionary generation were turning 69. In 1772, the oldest of the Awakeners were turning 71. Such visionary elders provide principled direction during the upheaval and hold up a vision of hope for the promised land. So in 1776 the peers of Benjamin Franklin in the pulpits called on heaven to bless the American cause, and gray-haired councils enacted blue laws in towns and colonies to keep Americans outwardly moral and Sabbath-honoring. More disturbing, they led vandalizing night raids on churches and homes of clergy suspected of loyalty to England. (Their disdain of the Anglicans was so severe that the denomination—later the Episcopal Church—was reduced from Colonial prominence to insignificance among American Protestants for 50 years.)

When the crisis turns out well—independence is won and the U.S. Constitution is enacted; fascism is destroyed and Western values are defended—elder Idealists are seen by younger generations as wise and passionate prophets, justified by history. They receive deference and honor and are viewed as matriarchs and patriarchs of their communities.

Younger generations regard them as the sages among us and heed these patriarchs' and matriarchs' fiery words, their recounting of recent glory, and hope for a blessing upon their young lives. These aged generations will want to minister to their juniors with words of inspiration and visions of hope, and younger generations will be inclined to accept such words from them.

But what happens when the crisis ends in tragedy, not triumph? Strauss and Howe point to the Civil War cycle of just three generations as the exception to their four-generation pattern.[19] The Transcendentalist generation of Idealists (Thoreau, Elizabeth Stanton, Lincoln, Jefferson Davis) brought on a national crisis in 1860 (oldest members of the Transcendentalists: 69). South Carolina's militant slaveholders saw the election of Lincoln as reason enough to secede from the United States. Idealists on both sides blessed their troops and condemned the other side. The casualties on both sides—Americans all—were horrific, and the destruction, especially in the South, was massive.

The upshot after the war was the complete discrediting of this generation with its dreams and ideals. In the South, leaders like Confederate President Jefferson Davis, and Vice President Alexander Stephens were imprisoned, fled to foreign parts, or passed into irrelevance. Their dreams of a slave-based way of life were shattered. But in the North too this generation was sidelined. The Transcendentalists had enough influence and power to add the 13th, 14th, and 15th Amendments to the Constitution, but the will to enforce racial equality was lost. Abolitionists like Senator Thaddeus Stevens were triumphant in their destruction of slavery, but they were quickly voted out of office by the scarred Gilded generation, who were Nomads who had done most of the bleeding.[20] The Gilded group saw these elders as fearsome and dangerous, despite the significance or nobility of their causes, and moved to wrest power from them.

If the historical and generational patterns Strauss and Howe have observed hold in the coming decades, we can expect a crisis beginning around 2010 and lasting until the middle of the 2020s. (Chapter 12 looks at this crisis era more closely.) If the outcome of this crisis is positive, we can expect Boomers in elderhood to receive honor and respect deep into their old age like other Idealist generations before them. The admonition of Leviticus, "You shall rise before the aged and defer to the old" (19:32) will come into vogue again.

On the other hand, if the outcome is negative, we can expect furious debates among the Boomers as to who was at fault. Younger generations may well close their ears to any wisdom such elders have to offer, and these seniors in such a situation may be burdened by guilt or still defiant. Either way, parish leaders will need to find ways to console these elders while also keeping peace between them and younger generations.

Dying and Legacy

Having lived a life seeking (and often finding) spiritual experiences and repeatedly sensing the nearness of God, Idealist generations typically face death with equanimity. Boomers can expect their spirituality to provide them with a sense of peace and serenity. Many will write poetry and prose about the meaning of their lives. Whatever causes have moved them, they will want younger generations to know, understand, and live by those causes. Asked by a Philadelphian in 1787 what the Constituting Convention had produced, Ben Franklin answered, "A Republic, madam—" and then added sharply: "If you can keep it."[21]

By the 2040s most of the Boomers will have died. How they will be remembered and how they will be treated in their ebbing years will depend on their leadership in the coming 20 years. What hopes and dreams will they set before younger generations? What word will they bring down from some contemporary Mount Sinai that will make them remembered far in the future? It will be fascinating to watch.

CHAPTER 7

MAKING THE BEST OF IT

Strauss and Howe's third generational type is the Nomad (a term they use in their later works, and one that I prefer to their earlier term "Reactive," as noted in the preface). Following in the wake of the visionary Idealists, Nomads find their life stages very different from those of other types. Strauss and Howe identify the generations within the Nomad type by the following dates and names.

NOMAD GENERATIONS	
Birth Years	Name used by Strauss & Howe
1961-1982	X
1883-1900	Lost
1822-1842	Gilded
1724-1741	Liberty
1615-1647	Cavalier

Youth

A time comes in the generational cycle when it seems that all the bad things that *could* happen, *do* happen. They happen to the generations Strauss and Howe call Nomads. As Generation X was born in the 1960s and 1970s, and as exhilarating, freeing or cathartic as those years were for parenting-age adults, they were hell for kids. In the name of freedom, children were freely exposed to all sorts of harsh realities at a very young age: divorce; unstable living-together arrangements; juvenile gangs that beat, robbed and even murdered; and crumbling, even physically dangerous, schools.

Growing Up Fast

As "Sesame Street" debuted in the late 1960s, Kermit the Frog endeared himself to a generation of children with his anthem "It's Not Easy Being Green." It's not easy being a child in a Nomadic generation. Family life is notoriously unstable and shifting. Many Generation Xers watched their parents go through divorce battles as children of the highest divorce rates of the 20th century.[1] These latchkey kids came out of their bedrooms to find strangers at the breakfast table[2] who had spent the night with single-again Mom or Dad.

Likewise, Cavalier generation children throughout England were orphaned by the thousands as their fathers fell in battle between Cromwell's Roundheads and the Royalists. Villages put to the torch drove thousands more orphans to the cities, where they scrambled for a living begging, sought out each other in gangs for protection, and were kidnapped (a word as yet uninvented) off the streets and sent by boatloads to the American colonies.[3]

Generation X's health indicators fell during Xers' youth and adolescence. Child and teen suicide rates rose to levels per capita not seen in 80 years (when the Lost generation Nomads were in *their* youth[4]). As the AIDS epidemic spread in the 1980s, its casualties were overwhelmingly from Generation X.

So it had been in the early 18th century Liberty generation. Colonial newspapers noted the rising number of children abandoned as bastards, turned over to wet nurses, fed liquor to quiet them, or left free to run around on their own.[5] An outbreak of diphtheria claimed between 5 and 10 percent of children in half the colonies in the 1730s and 1740s.[6] Thousands of others succumbed to smallpox as children, adolescents, and adults.

School

Things were no better for Generation X in school. A mass emigration of teachers out of the profession into better-paying jobs left behind increasing class sizes and "a rising tide of mediocrity," as the Department of Education described the nation's schools in 1983. Elementary students and teens brought more than a half-million knives a day to school in urban neighborhoods.[7]

Gen X students, like other Nomads before them, responded by quitting school and joining the workforce (charted by the Department of Labor's steady rise in the number of child-labor law violations[8]). For the 1883–1900 Lost generation, the percentage of white elementary students fell by 8 percentage points. In the same years the number of newsboys and shoeshine boys in major cities rose to one-sixth of all school-age students.[9] When Nomads of the Gilded generation reached their college-age years, they left in droves for the California gold rush and the New England whaling fleets. Operating the dazzling new telegraphs or working as a conductor for the spreading network of railroads seemed more lucrative options than studying Latin verbs or British poets.

Attitudes

In 1987 when Boomer Bill Bennett, social critic and public scold, excoriated the next-younger generation and called for a return to virtue and character formation, he followed in the footsteps of earlier Idealists viewing the next-younger generation. Midlife New Englanders in the mid-17th century spoke routinely of a corrupt and degenerate rising generation—or, as Puritan Richard Mather put it, "the sad face of the rising generation."[10] Lost generation actor W. C. Fields's famous line, "Any man who hates children and dogs can't be all bad," reminded his peers of adult attitudes toward the Lost when they were children.

Hollywood both reflected and reinforced a negative view of Generation X. In the 1960s and 1970s directors and producers found a solid market for films featuring children as dangerous, even murderous. Wholesome, family-friendly Disney turned from animated features to theme parks for corporate revenues (opening Florida's Disney World in 1971).

Faith Matters

Religion is not immune from childhood upheaval. Nomad children have often received spotty religious instruction and find little comfort in their congregational settings. Their (mostly Adaptive) parents were committed to expanding options and choices. For Adaptives, bringing children to Sunday school or Torah study every single week felt too much like their own stringent childhood. In the name of freedom children were left to decide on their own if and when they attended worship and religious instruction. During the 1960s and 1970s denominations that routinely practice infant baptism repeatedly heard Silent parents say, "I'm not going to have the [Generation X] baby baptized. I'll let the kid make that choice on her own later on." (This attitude also gave Silent parents freedom—from an obligation.)

Denied a consistent core of beliefs, and steadily moved in and out of religious instruction, Nomad generations end up with a patchwork of religious experiences that often lack coherence. Four Catholic Christmas Eve masses, two Presbyterian Easter services, six months of Torah-Talmud instruction, a year in a Hindu commune, and three two-week vacation Bible schools among the Lutherans do not add up to a firm spiritual foundation for a hypothetical high school senior.

As a result, Nomads grow up wary and skeptical of religion. These generations encounter much pain in their lives, and they focus their attention on the world around them, alert for the next possible threat. They spend little time on inward exploration because self-protection comes first—protecting oneself from outside dangers. With worldly dangers all around, they typically develop a strong sense of outward-focused realism. This realism clashes sharply with many of the "unreal" aspects of faith. Prayer to an unseen God and the spiritual benefits of religion often sound like a scam to Nomad ears.

Now there is a faithful remnant in every generation, and Nomads are no exception. When they *are* touched by the power of God, and they *experience* God's acceptance and forgiveness, their embrace of the faith can be dramatic. A congregation can help keep such converts in a faith relationship. A faith mentor who has been scarred by life and healed by God's work will be perceived as authentic by Nomads. Nomad converts are often eager to explore their new faith, so besides mentors, a congregation can also provide more formal instruction. Such instruction will need to be carefully designed with an emphasis on practicality, or new Nomad converts might perceive such instruction and the faith as inauthentic and unreal.

Toward the end of Nomads' youth, the economy performs erratically. Stagflation, bank panics, and various crises punctuate the end of a postwar expansion and middle-class growth. They also signal the Nomads on the brink of joining the adult labor force that they will continue to need their wits and other survival skills. No one seems to play by the rules anymore, so the new workers are left making up their own rules and finding their own way.

Rising Adulthood

Nomad generations face the debris of an upheaval—social, economic, and cultural. Members frequently form small groups for survival and protection. For Nomads, a small circle of friends who share a common music, outlook, and survival methods functions almost as a surrogate family. Generation Xers use instant messaging to stay connected with their circle, and have made "Friends" a top television hit. More negatively, these groups can become gangs like the West Coast-based Bloods and Crips, or the Wild West outlaws of the Gilded generation. Such gangs use Nomad survival skills for cunning criminal acts.

Working

As Generation Xers entered the work force during the 1980s, they lived in a kinetic economy of on-line day trading, incessant Fortune 500 layoffs, wide-open start-up possibilities and varied job résumés. Unlike the postwar boom of the 1950s, with its bursting middle class, this era's economic growth was uneven. The rich grew fabulously wealthy while the middle class only moved ahead modestly. (From 1982 to 1996, compensation of the roughly 1,000 presidents and CEOs of the Fortune 500 companies grew from 40 times to 240 times their average employee's compensation.[11]) Like the fictional Jack Dawson of 1912 in the movie *Titanic*—a young man who worked odd jobs from port to port on tramp steamers—Generation Xers often face a paycheck-to-paycheck existence and a precariousness in jobs unknown to older generations. With a few dazzling exceptions they are worse off financially at their present age than any other living American generation.

Risk-taking entrepreneurs among Nomads test (or break) all the existing economic and business rules, experiment with new technology, and explore or create their own niches. For Xers, so far there have been a few spectacular economic winners, like Michael Dell (computers), Jeff Bezos (Amazon.com) and Steve Case (America Online). Many more Xers have put in 16-hour workdays at start-up dot.coms that resulted in nothing except another résumé entry.

Economic pressures and a survival mentality make Generation Xers a hardworking generation, but they work differently from the Boomers ahead of them. The Boomers retooled the economy along 24/7 lines and now *live to work*. They invented abominations like the "working vacation" and boast how long it has been since they took time off. They often bring home a company laptop and use cell phones incessantly to check in at the office.

Generation Xers work hard, maybe holding down two part-time jobs with no benefits, and may keep a folding cot tucked away on one side of the cubicle. But when they are off, they are gone. They *work to live*, and are sharpening the distinction between work and home. Cell phones with caller ID lets them keep in touch with friends and screen corporate calls.

Social Issues and Reactions

Playing by the rules often doesn't work for Nomads, so they look for ways to beat the system or to get a lucky break. In their rising adulthood, gambling blooms across the country. Pitch-and-toss games filled the taverns and emptied the pockets of the Liberty generation.[12] Riverboat gamblers and saloon poker players preyed on other members of the Gilded generation. Computerized state lotteries and tribal casinos pluck the dollars of Generation X.

Given the bleak outlook Nomad generations have faced in life, it is not surprising that many turned to drinking or drug abuse to dull the pain of life. In the 1750s West Indies molasses was imported and brewed into rum. This Colonial favorite was consumed locally in vast amounts and exported widely throughout the British Empire. In 1750, Massachusetts alone was exporting more than 2 million gallons a year.[13] (Total American population in the 13 colonies at the time was about 2.5 million.) The turn-of-the-20th-century Lost not only drank; they also dulled their pain with new chemicals like opium, heroin, and cocaine (this last a common ingredient in cough syrups and, until 1904, in Coca-Cola).

While such mood-altering chemicals become popular for Idealists in their own rising adulthood, in midlife Idealists begin crusades against the chemicals abused by the next-younger Nomads. British officials tried taxing the rum trade. An unsuccessful American experiment in national Prohibition began in 1920 with passage of a constitutional amendment.

Nomad generations react with fury and subterfuge. Riots rocked Colonial towns and cities as British troops tried to shut down taverns that were behind in their tax payments. Meanwhile, the Liberty generation's John Hancock made a tidy fortune smuggling in untaxed molasses in his ships from the Caribbean and smuggling out untaxed rum to the British Empire. Sometimes Nomads react with sheer defiance. One Ohio winery, reduced to selling only grape juice during Prohibition in the 1920s, carefully labeled each bottle: "Warning! Do NOT add 1/2 cup of sugar and 1 packet of yeast to this bottle and leave in a cupboard for three weeks. This produces a violation of federal law."[14]

A significant percentage of Nomad generations enter the military and make a career of it. The military provides an ordered environment (in contrast with the chaos of Nomads' early life), and a chance for using their survival and improvisational skills to the limit. Generation X is unusual in that the military has been a volunteer organization all their lives. So far Generation Xers' involvement in actual fighting has been of the brushfire variety with extremely low casualties—invading Grenada, capturing Panamanian dictator Manuel Noriega, being deployed to Lebanon, Somalia, and Bosnia for peacekeeping operations. The largest action to date has been the Gulf War, and losses were hearteningly small.

By contrast, earlier Nomad generations in rising adulthood have been engaged in larger operations and have often been badly led and needlessly sacrificed. Most tragically, the Civil War-era Gilded generation stands out among all American generations for all the wrong reasons. Ulysses S. Grant, James Longstreet (Robert E. Lee's most reliable corps commander), Stonewall Jackson, and many others of this generation's first wave earned their stripes as junior officers in the Mexican War of 1846–1848. But they were called back to fight each other in the Civil War. Then each side's capacity for killing the other's soldiers (mostly younger members of their own Gilded generation) swamped what medical knowledge and skill existed. Civil War soldiers' suffering was almost beyond modern imagining.

Religion

Members of Nomad generations will take a hard look at our fill-in-the-blank sentence, "God is _____." Having lived by their wits all their lives and strongly self-reliant, Nomads look reality in the eye and insist that the faith not be sugarcoated. They often measure authenticity by the presence of suffering. They will tentatively or perhaps skeptically tend to complete the statement as "God *can persuade me*." If overtly religious people are breezily optimistic or quick to offer easy answers to knotty questions, they will repel Nomads. But Nomads find realistic the scriptures that express lamentation over suffering (like Job or Jeremiah). A God who endures injustice and pain (as Jesus did in Holy Week) sounds authentic, and so worthy of their attention, and worthy to be the center of their faith.

Israel's first king, Saul, seems to typify Nomad leadership. Saul is taken from a donkey-hunting expedition (1 Sam. 9) and made king. He does not feel himself worthy of the task (1 Sam. 10:21-23), an opinion shared by others (v. 27). His reign is marked by continual warfare, against both external enemies like the Philistines and internal rivals like David. He is self-reliant and rule-breaking to a fault, offering a sacrifice for victory that only the prophet Samuel was meant to do (1 Sam. 13: 5-14), ignoring clear commands of how to treat his enemies (1 Sam. 15), and turning away from Israel's God to other powers (1 Sam. 29: 3-19). He and his house pay for his headstrong rashness by all dying in battle (1 Sam. 31).

As young adults Nomads are risk-taking at work; well acquainted with pain, suffering, and disappointment; protective at home; and skeptical about what is not real. Yet, in more cases than might be thought, they will consider what God might mean in their lives. Strongly traditional congregations and religious leaders who highly value order and heritage can find it hard to connect with this spontaneous, in-the-moment generation. Congregations that wish to welcome Generation X and religious leaders who want to minister to them will need to modify, retool, and even abandon several cherished assumptions about how things work around a congregation.

Consider the central focus of a congregation, the worship service. Worship is a major entry point to a congregation for Generation Xers, but unless a congregation has made some of the following changes in its worship service, visiting Xers will not return.

- Martin Luther called the church a "mouth house," and many worship services are quite verbal. Generation X is visually oriented, so movement and colors are appealing.
- To attract Generation Xers, worship needs to be interactive, with everyone joining in beyond standing, sitting, and singing. Congregations with a freer worship style are more interactive, with praise choruses, projected and continuously shifting visual images, and talk-show-style interviews. More liturgical congregations expect the laity to play their part in the liturgy, which is a set form of interaction. (When the congregation makes responses that are not printed or noted, but that

"everyone just knows," outsiders and visitors unfortunately are excluded.) Liturgical congregations at times have been more interactive than they know with a candlelight Christmas Eve service when everyone carries a candle and with its flame lights a neighbor's candle. A Palm Sunday processional with the whole congregation marching around the worship space waving palm branches is interactive.

- Sermons need to be interactive as well. Of course making a connection between the preacher and the people is a weekly challenge for clergy. Preaching that connects with Generation Xers can include drama, film clips, and PowerPoint presentations. Partway through a sermon on a familiar parable, an invitation to take part raises everyone's participation level: "Who would you call a good Samaritan today? I invite you to turn to someone else in the pews and exchange ideas about who you've heard of who might be a good Samaritan." Inviting feedback a few minutes later, as a Minneapolis pastor does, and incorporating some of it into the rest of the sermon or service, is particularly effective interaction.

- This tech-savvy, MP3-player generation has one interpretation of *silence* or of a *lack of movement*: something is wrong or broken. Worship leaders can address this viewpoint in two ways. One is to quicken the pace of the service and reduce silence to a minimum. While some longtime members may object, many others will appreciate a livelier tempo. Another, more difficult way is for worship leaders, clergy, and teachers to begin educating the congregation about the history, uses, and significance of deep silence. Materials and resources on forms of prayer will help leaders address this challenge.

- A few times a year leaders should offer a running commentary on every part of the service (either spoken or projected on a screen or wall). Generation Xers have often had only haphazard worship exposure, and they simply *do not know* what is happening or why. (Longtime members will often learn more from such Sunday commentaries than they are willing to admit.)

- This lack of background also means that a congregation and its leaders cannot use any religious language or abbreviations until they are explained. Denominational alphabet soup—SBC, BVM, LBW, for example—is also bewildering. (SBC is Southern Baptist Convention; BVM, Blessed Virgin Mary; LBW, Lutheran Book of Worship.) Consider how a few of the following terms can strike members of Generation X.

Religious term	Generation X understanding
Apostle	A recent movie title
Corporate	Where Xers work; Fortune 500 list
Confession	When the perp tells police how she committed a crime
Creed	Name of a band
Hymn	Misspelled opposite of "her"
Kyrie/Kyrie Eleison	Good song from *Mister-Mister* in the 1980s
Preaching	Moralizing, finger-wagging, and condemnation
Trespass(es)	Walking on somebody's land without permission
Virgin Birth	"Well, yeah. We're all born virgins."
Witness	Person who saw a crime

If Generation X members join your congregation, one thing you can do is to design classes that fill in some of their religious blank spots. Xers are the ones making the "Alpha" classes (developed in England for unchurched young adults) into an international, cross-denominational phenomenon. But classes about your denomination and your congregation will help too, especially if they are action-oriented and interactive. Nomad generations often become the new denominational stalwarts.

Other classes and courses that provide various life skills are also a good strategy. Again, "class" should be understood loosely, as a session designed with interactive components and physical action (kinesthetic learning).

- Premarital classes with some real depth, with input from other Gen X married couples.
- Marriage enrichment courses for building relationships and strengthening marriages. Many in this generation saw their parents unhappy and divorced and are determined that their own marriage will be different and better.
- Parenting classes. Xers often make common cause with the dominant Boomers for the sake of their children. Nomad generations have a history of protecting those younger than themselves because they don't want anyone else going through what they went through. Gen Xers

will know a number of things to avoid as parents, but will appreciate being filled in on things to do.

- Financial organizing and planning. Survival means a lot to Nomads, and money is a means of survival. Money-management classes, especially when these are updated to use the computer home finance program Quicken and a Palm Pilot, are helpful.
- Home repair and maintenance. As strapped for cash as this generation often is, some type of hands-on, money-saving classes will be well received. Congregation members with appropriate skills can serve as teachers.
- Mother's Day Out and Dad's Day Out. Newly married Nomad couples both work and save hard for the down payment on their first home, but then one becomes the stay-at-home parent. In a surprising number of cases this is *Dad*. Many congregations already have regular Mother's Day Out events, with Bible study, or an outing, or a guest speaker, or simply a half-day respite for mothers, all with child care provided. Cutting-edge congregations reaching this generation would do well designing and offering a Dad's Day Out program. As with the women, providing quality child care is the key piece.

Nomads do all sorts of dirty work on the job, in social settings, and in the culture at large. They do not often get thanked—a courtesy which religious bodies could purposely extend to their Nomad volunteers. If you ask some of the techno-savvy types to network the congregation's computer systems and tie them into a broadband cable modem, and you need it done on a deadline, they'll do it. Fuel for the effort could be pizza and soft drinks, and thanks could take the form of a gift certificate from an on-line book store.

This is not the generation whose members should be put on a committee. (They don't like hearing about Silent generation process or procedure, and they are less than thrilled listening to Boomers argue and moralize.) If a group must be formed, make it a task force, with a specific, measurable goal and deadline. Generation X will show up for the Habitat for Humanity building project, make time for the Adopt-a-Highway clean-up, or help convert four Sunday School rooms into temporary sleeping quarters for a week for homeless families.

Stewardship

Religious leaders who lead stewardship efforts will find Generation X facing a different set of circumstances than other generations in the congregation. Generation X in 2002 ranges in age from 20 to 41, meaning virtually all of its members are in rising adulthood. They are getting married, starting families, considering economic possibilities, and taking chances. People of any generation in this stage of life find discretionary income at its minimum because of the start-up costs of adulthood. School debts, wedding expenses, a security deposit for an apartment, the down payment on a house, maternity medical bills, and the costs of caring for a baby are the heavy financial obligations in this stage of life.

Nomad generations historically have had the fewest resources and the least help in coping with these economic pressures. Younger members of Generation X are just entering the workforce, so they are in entry-level, low-paying jobs. The federal minimum wage has not kept pace with the cost of living. State and local efforts to provide a minimum living wage have generally been defeated. As the newest workers, Xers are also on the bottom side of the two-tier wage systems many companies have imposed on their work forces. Better wages, benefits, and a measure of job security go to the old hands. The new hires receive the legal minimum of everything and are the first to be dismissed in an economic slowdown.

Generation X has proportionately the highest personal debt loads and the leanest prospects of any current generation.[15] The 401(k) and IRA plans boom as Xers scrimp for their own retirements. They have taken to heart the doomsday scenarios about Social Security and believe they have to get ready for old age on their own. (One poll shows that 21 percent of Generation X members believe in the existence of UFOs and extraterrestrials, while only 5 percent believe that they will receive *anything* from Social Security.[16])

Generation Xers also cope by bartering. They get things done by trading services, as Internet sites post offers like "Will trade installing T-1 line and LAN for up to 12 stations for installation of kitchen cabinets and counter tops." Or, less technologically, one parent might propose to another: "I'll give your kid harp lessons if you'll give mine driving lessons."

Gen Xers are hardworking on the job, hard-playing off the job, seeking balance in life and something beyond just survival. They are careful but quick and decisive. They tend toward the laconic and will play their cards close to the vest. As a rule (though with many exceptions), they are action-oriented and surprisingly skilled in unsuspected ways.

The Stewardship Request

Congregational stewardship leaders really have to live and breathe the idea that stewardship means treasure, *time, and talents*. Xers often do *not* have income or resources for a sizable pledge or gift (although what they do give is often more sacrificial than for many parishioners.) Congregational leaders should strive for a congregational culture that truly embraces the idea that people can make their contribution in currency other than money. Leaders need to develop creative and innovative ways of recognizing gifts of time and talent. Especially for this generation, volunteering time and having a chance to put talents and skills to work are authentic expressions of their stewardship.

- In many cases members of this generation will invite you into their homes. They are often intensely proud of the work they have done rehabbing or renovating their quarters. Comments about how much work has gone into the project and how it looks to be a safe and cozy haven may set a good tone.
- Be brief to the point of bluntness. (This approach can be hard for the Silent generation.) Stick to the main core and central themes and avoid details or nuances. If a Generation Xer wants more information, he'll ask. The reply should err on the side of terseness.
- Children's issues and needs, particularly children's safety, go over big with this young parent generation. Generation X really wants a congregation to be a safe place—physically, emotionally, relationally, and spiritually. If you have (or are starting) a day-care center, emphasize the *stability* of the staff compared to staffing in commercial day-care operations. Daily feedback reports to parents—about the child's motor skills, language development, social interactions, and so forth—convey safety and quality to Xer parents.
- Mention the youth program, especially the ways kids get real-world, hands-on experience through service projects. A vivid description of the grinding poverty at an Indian reservation, coupled with what our youth and three carpenters from our congregation did to lend a hand

(insulating walls, rebuilding porches, putting on a vacation Bible school for the younger kids) will go over well.

- An emphasis on continuing or planned life-skill classes, retreats, and programs will be well received. Financial management, home budgeting, Christian parenting, baby-sitter training through the Red Cross, and Marriage Encounter weekends for couples are examples of such classes for this generation.
- The congregational Web site ought to be mentioned at least once, along with its address.
- If the congregation has an automatic deduction plan, using electronic funds transfer as a method of taking a member's contribution, it's worth mentioning. Members of this generation often have several regular automatic deposits and withdrawals from their bank accounts. While they may not sign up to give their pledge this way, they will be impressed that you have it as an option. It adds to the congregation's "cool quotient."
- Note physical plant or equipment replacements or upgrades that are coming. Anything low-tech that is being upgraded so that people have the tools to do a better job will have solid appeal.

The Approach of Midlife

Historically, as the leading-edge members of Nomad generations have approached 50 (for Xers, somewhere short of 2011), American society has been hit by a crisis. As the generation in midlife and taking leadership in such times, Nomad generations face the emergency as parents, workers, citizens, and people of faith. Nomads' survival instincts, pluck, persistence, and even rule-breaking serve them well in coping.

Parenting and Schools

As parents in such a crisis, Nomad parents first focus on protecting their children. Physically they sacrifice for food, clothing, and shelter—working a second job, taking in laundry, planting a vegetable garden, sending home all of a soldier's pay. In more dire circumstances children may be sent to better-off relatives.

Emotionally, Nomad parents have stared despair in the face, but they work hard to spare or shield their children from fear, panic, and dread.

Under enormous pressure in the larger world, they often suppress their own feelings at home to keep their children from being scarred. Child nurture swings past protection toward smothering as children are taught obedience, cooperation, and deference. Parents make it clear that adults are making great sacrifices on their behalf, that life is hard now but will be better for the children and youth later.

In schools Nomad generations structure their children's world with authoritative but kind teachers and administrators. Specialists on staff disappear unless they provide immediate practical instruction (for example, shop teachers). Coursework veers toward the practical, rather than knowledge for its own sake. Pragmatic and innovative application is prized, like building a radio set out of tin cans, spare wire, and a half-used car battery. Achievement is encouraged, expected, and rewarded.

Truancy is not tolerated and is vigorously punished. Child labor laws are strongly enforced (the scarcity of jobs of any kind also closes off this attraction.) Admission to schools for previously excluded students or for migrant children is handled case by case by local administrators, not by legislation or lawsuits. When such students are admitted, teachers and principals brook no teasing or scorn that they detect from other children (or their parents). When they are excluded (for space reasons, but at times for prejudicial ones) little formal protest is heard from parents or others.

Leadership

This protection of the young goes beyond parenting. Protecting those in their charge becomes a hallmark of Nomad generations, on the grounds that "no one should have to go through what I went through at that age." Fans of the TV sitcom "M*A*S*H" will know the character Colonel Sherman Potter of the Lost generation. Presiding over a unit that is a cross between a hospital and a circus, Potter is fearless in defending his people against generals, CIA men, or rear-echelon bureaucrats who want more discipline.

Catholic Bishop John Ireland of St. Paul, Minnesota (Gilded generation), held the office in the 1880s and 1890s, when a huge wave of East European Catholics flooded the Upper Midwest. Ireland defended his flock against religious and nativist bigots, who feared that the immigrants' numbers would overwhelm "true Americans" and Protestant power. He also fended off his Roman superiors, who found his Catholicism becoming too American.

Not only do Nomads protect their juniors, but they also treat them with kindness. Bishop Ireland marshaled Catholics to set up hospitals, orphanages, and parochial schools for immigrants. He insisted that children and their parents learn English so they would have a critical tool for higher education and economic opportunity.

When the British surrendered at Yorktown, led out by their second-in-command (Cornwallis chickened out), Washington directed that the Britisher surrender his sword to Benjamin Lincoln. Lincoln was an American general who had been humiliated by his surrender of Charleston to the British the year before, so Washington gave him the honor of receiving the surrender.[17]

A business-savvy generation, Nomads bring that expertise to their faith communities, often shocking older Idealists and troubling pietists who want a sharp separation of religion and business. Evangelist Dwight L. Moody (Gilded) began his ministry in Chicago by first *renting* the back four pews from an existing church so that he could lead his own worship services whenever his landlord wasn't using the space. His award-winning sales skills helped him fill those pews on Sundays, mostly with his fellow Gilded generation members from the streets and boarding houses. Soon after, Moody's own Illinois Street congregation of the poor struggled for some time as it operated without denominational backing. It began thriving financially when he secured the financial support of businessmen like inventor Cyrus McCormick and meatpacker George Armour.[18] Moody sold them on the idea of backing a church they wouldn't consider attending.

Religious Leadership

Nomad religious figures from earlier generations reflect many of the traits just noted. The list of exemplars of Generation X is rather short because they are rather young (in 2002) and have not had much time to make their mark.

TABLE OF NOTABLE RELIGIOUS NOMADS

Years	Name	Contribution
1643–1729	Solomon Stoddard	Puritan theologian who successfully argued that the baptized but un-regenerate (those without a spiritual conversion) should be admitted to the Lord's Supper on grounds that they needed it for their spiritual health.
1644–1718	William Penn	Wealthy adventurer, convert to Quakerism in 1667. Founder of Pennsylvania. All denominations and sects welcomed, expected to cooperate in civil society.
1645(?)–1711	Eusibio Kino	Jesuit explorer, builder of San Xavier del Bac mission in Tucson in 1697.
1649–1721	Elihu Yale	Wealthy trader; in 1700 was asked for major contribution to found a Connecticut university and school for training clergy. Had money to give and gave it.
1723–1794	John Witherspoon	President, Princeton University (Presbyterian). Only ordained signer of Declaration of Independence. Secured books for the library and science equipment for students to practice applying their studies.
1735–1815	John Carroll	Along with cousin Charles (signer of Declaration), rallied Roman Catholics to Patriot cause in Revolution, defusing much Protestant antagonism. Appointed first bishop in U.S., Baltimore, in 1789.
1738–1789	Ethan Allen	Green Mountain boys leader, captured Fort Ticonderoga in 1775. Author, *Reason, the Only Oracle of Man* (1784), Deist viewpoint, very much opposed to revealed religion.

1835–1910	Samuel Langhorne Clemens	The beloved Mark Twain—author, sharp-tongued humorist, and religious skeptic.
1837–1899	Dwight L. Moody	Congregationalist layman and preacher. Distributed Bibles to Union troops; founded Illinois Street congregation (Chicago), Moody Bible Institute, and Moody Press.
1838–1918	John Ireland	Roman Catholic archbishop of St. Paul (1888). Instrumental in freeing American Catholicism from foreign influence. Insisted on English only in parochial schools to help immigrants integrate and find jobs and opportunities.
1839–1902	Michael Corrigan	Irish Roman Catholic archbishop of New York City. Established and expanded parochial schools, orphanages, and hospitals for immigrants.
1890–1944	Aimee Semple McPherson	Founder, International Four Square Businessman's Gospel Tabernacle in 1920s. Survived sex scandal and financial irregularities.
1892–1973	Reinhold Niebuhr	Evangelical and Reformed theologian, self-proclaimed Christian realist. Author, *Moral Man and Immoral Society* (1952).
1895–1979	Fulton J. Sheen	Catholic bishop and host of weekly network TV program, "Life is Worth Living" (1951–1957). Patient defender and explainer of Catholicism to Protestant America.
1898–1993	Norman Vincent Peale	Reformed Church of America minister, author of *The Power of Positive Thinking* (1952).
1962–	Steven C. Chapman	Christian musician, founder "Jars of Clay" band, 14 albums released, beginning in 1992.

1964–	Yolanda Adams	Contemporary African American Gospel singer, four albums since 1997; Grammy winner.
1968–	Todd Hahn	Presbyterian pastor, pioneer in developing post-modern forms of worship designed for Generation X. Author, *Reckless Hope: Understanding and Reaching Baby Busters* (1996), *GenXers after God: Helping a Generation Pursue Jesus* (1998).
1969–	Tom Beaudoin	Catholic professor at Boston College, and author; *Virtual Faith: The Irreverent Spiritual Quest of Generation X* (1998), *Proclaiming the Gospel in a Wired World* (2001).

Having come warily to the faith, Nomad converts often embrace religion with zeal. They do not forget their wariness, however, and as leaders they respect people (especially younger ones) who creep up on the faith slowly. Nomad religious leaders are much more action-oriented than word-oriented. If there is trouble in the community (danger, joblessness, chaos, or crisis), they don't protest, or begin crusades against the causes of the trouble. Nomads are the embodiment of faith *active* in love. Lost generation clergy formed unusual (for the time) alliances across denominational and even religious boundaries to help people cope with crises. Catholic soup kitchens served poor Baptists; Presbyterian clergy passed on rumors of jobs to the Jewish families down the street; the Salvation Army provided sleeping quarters for Lutheran and Methodist drifters.

At this stage of life Nomads move into leadership in religious circles and across society. Nomad leaders are alert to threats and are masters of improvisation. Their solutions tend to be inventive, practical, and immediate. Nomad generations have been forced to live in the moment all their lives. Nomads perceive their context with realism, while their pragmatism lets them adapt to almost any situation. Historically they have also been America's most diverse generations, so making cross-cultural connections has been a necessity for them. In midlife they are the ones on the spot when the latest American crisis has hit, and they have risen to the challenge. The one time the crisis came early and they were not in charge (the Civil War cycle, covered more fully in chapters 8 and 12), things went rather badly.

Communication

Nomad leaders have been characteristically plainspoken, straightforward, and generally humble, and they don't put on airs. They are like George Washington as the nation's first president. Many in Congress and the Cabinet debated how the new leader should be addressed. "Your Excellency" and "His Excellency" were among the titles bandied about, as well as a congressional committee proposal of "His Highness, the President of the United States and Protector of the Rights of the Same." Washington brought the discussions to a close with his insistence on a simple "Mr. President."[19]

Likewise, Generation X as communicators and preachers will tend to be on the blunt, plainspoken, and unvarnished side, but also display a memorable wit. (A generational type that contains a Mark Twain, a Groucho Marx, a Charlie Chaplin, and a Mae West will have some members with a breathtaking sense of humor.) They will resemble the Lost generation's Babe Ruth, who in 1930 (as the Depression crushed the country) was given a contract for $80,000. A reporter pointed out that this was more money than the U.S. president was making and asked if Ruth didn't feel a bit squeamish about accepting such a sum. The Babe replied, "I had a better year than the President."[20]

Nomad church leaders would perhaps interpret the parable of the Good Samaritan along these lines:

> It seems that the priest and the Levite are too busy or preoccupied with their work to lend a hand. But the Samaritan sees—really sees—this mugging victim, a nasty, bloody sight. Now the Samaritan is no emergency medical technician, but he goes into action anyway. He pours on wine and oil, and bandages up the guy. He loads him onto his own donkey and takes him to an inn, like a Super 8, and settles the guy in.
>
> And you know, I suspect the Samaritan might not look so good to the innkeeper, because in this era Jews and Samaritans are almost like rival gang members. He doubts that the innkeeper will keep his word. So the Samaritan offers him a cash incentive to do what needs to be done. With luck, it all works out.

Xers will be practical communicators with pragmatic solutions. Historically Nomads have brought a new emphasis to denominational distinctions. This is a function of their often dramatic embrace of the faith. Having been skeptical for so long, when they embrace a faith tradition

Nomads frequently want to dig deeply into just what it means to be Catholic, Jewish, or Methodist. Yet this interest is usually contained within the congregation. Nomad members tend not to use these distinctions for divisions, preferring cooperation and action in the face of a crisis.

Future Elderhood

Looking back on Nomad generations over the past four centuries, we can make a few educated guesses about what elderhood will be like for Generation X, and how religious groups can do ministry with them, and be blessed by them.

Nomads have found that life gives them few favors, and so in old age they don't look for them. (When Franklin Roosevelt launched a raft of alphabet-soup agencies to lift America out of the Depression, the Lost was the only generation not specifically targeted by a program.[21]) When Lost generation member Ethel Andrus founded the American Association of Retired People (AARP) in 1959, she was adamant about how it would and would not operate. She refused "to bewail the hardships of old age . . . nor to stress political strength of older folk, nor to urge governmental subsidy.[22]

As in their working lives, Nomads in retirement see the widest spread of economic circumstances of the four generational types and skewed toward the bottom of the economic ladder. It was probably a Nomad who coined the New England proverb "Use it up, wear it out, make it do, or do without." Given the frequent hardships such generations suffer in elderhood, religious groups can put their faith into action by even small gestures of aid for aged Nomads. (For example, a light bill paid from congregational funds in the 1970s; a wireless, broadband house network utility bill paid in the 2030s.)

Aging Nomad generations have often kept their personal focus on their immediate family. Their old-age living arrangements have usually followed suit. Even those of the Lost generation, who had the chance to get away from it all by moving to Florida, Arizona, and other Sunbelt spots in the 1960s, generally did not do so. Instead, a common Lost generation member was the old man in the neighborhood who spoke English funny, living in the one remaining farmhouse in a sea of Levittown look-alike ranch-style houses so that he could be near his daughter.

Congregations and faith-based groups will likely be able to do good work with the aging Xers in a couple of ways. (The first Xers will turn 65 in 2026, but the retirement age for Social Security is slated to be 67 by this time.) If Generation Xers stick close to family, then congregations and agencies can provide respite care for younger family members caring for often cantankerous retirees. Congregations could provide shopping and transportation for both family and retirees, and establish support groups among their members facing the same challenges.

Religious bodies might provide the 21st century equivalent of Meals on Wheels and visitation nurses. If people who come calling can speak the "old country" language, that skill will be a plus. (In the second quarter of the 21st century these languages would include Spanish, Lao, Hmong, Chinese, Korean, Arabic, and various dialects of Vietnamese, Serbian, Thai, and Urdu, among others.)

A disturbing pattern has prevailed of elder Nomads being neglected and ignored in their later years. In the 1790s, as Liberty generation members became seniors, New England churches eliminated age-ranked seating, and a majority of states imposed mandatory retirement ages for judges.[23] "Fogy," "curmudgeon," and "codger" are negative terms in common American parlance coined in the late 1700s just as the Liberty generation was entering elderhood.[24]

Here is a place where church, synagogue, mosque, and temple can lean against the prevailing winds of culture and remember senior Americans with honor. The culture in such times may be all agog over indulging youth and people in midlife building infrastructure, while old Nomads are seen as overcautious and timid, or as obstacles. But religious bodies can heed these elders, whose unflinching view of the best and worst of human nature can be a blessing.

Mark Twain at 63 looked on the war fever gripping the country on the verge of the Spanish-American War (1898), along with the proposed annexation of the Philippines. He saw through what was driving many of the hawks with the words, "I pray you pause and consider. Against our traditions we are now entering upon an unjust and trivial war, a war against a helpless people, and for a base object—robbery."[25] Younger generations ignored Twain and his peers and did just what he described. They used American might to rob Spain of Cuba and the Phillipines. Heeding Twain would have saved later American leaders a world of troubles and Latin American "Yánquí, go home!" headaches.

Religious judicatory officials who oversee a congregation in crisis could bless that situation by calling in retired Nomad clergy. Their keen realism and zest for crisis management mean they would get to the bottom of a situation quickly and insightfully. A trouble-making parishioner may well underestimate the kind old-timer the judicatory has sent over. Congregational alligators will be outflanked, disarmed, and put in their place in short order by such an interim pastor. Other members of the congregation who have been hurt will delight at such an able ministry.

Death and Legacy

Nomads have historically died at disproportionately high rates in their earlier years, so relatively fewer members of these hard-living, adventurous generations have died of natural causes.[26] Those who have found God in their lives often look forward to the hereafter. The promises of eternal rest have a particular appeal to such kinetic generations that have often been forced to live on the edge. Even Nomads outside the faith communities who are skeptics to the end look death in the eye with the same steady gaze as they have looked at life. Their unflinching, straight-from-the-shoulder attitude even toward dying arouses admiration in their loved ones.

Nomads (again, with a few spectacular exceptions) often leave little behind in their estates. Mostly this is a function of how little they were able to acquire, or hang on to, in the face of cruel financial pressures. They often leave what they have to family. There are surprises from time to time. Nomads sometimes adapt so fully to a life of scrimping that they live *below* their means, and their estates are surprisingly large. When they make bequests beyond the family circle, common recipients are charities, religious bodies, or other organizations that take direct action for those down on their luck.

In Nomad generations virtues of determination and courage, both put into action, shine out. Younger generations see embodied in Nomads what faith active in love means in human terms.

CHAPTER 8

ALL TOGETHER NOW

"Work hard, play by the rules, and everybody gets a reward."[1] Strauss and Howe in *Generations* call their final generational type the Civic. As with the other types, Civics have recurred several times through the generational cycles.

Birth Years	CIVICS Name used by Strauss & Howe
1983-2005	Millennials
1901-1924	GIs
1742-1766	Republicans
1648-1673	Glorious

In every generational cycle there comes a point when one of the generational types appears only among either the very old or the children . At the turn of the 21st century that generational type is the Civic. Members of the World War II veteran GI generation range in age from 78 to 101. They are dying of old age by the hundreds every day. At the other end of life, the new Millennial generation of Civics is adding 10,000 new members a day in hospital delivery rooms and "birthing suites" across America. Their oldest members are approaching their 20th birthdays.

So for now the Civic generational type is the one in adult eclipse. Studying this type means looking forward and backward in time more than for the other types. And in looking back along the list at the head of this chapter, readers will notice an odd omission. Strauss and Howe do not list a Civic generational type for the 19th century, an exception to their own four-generational pattern (noted earlier in chapters 6 and 7).

A social emergency seems to erupt in America on a rather regular basis. (This phenomenon will be examined more fully in chapter 12.) Strauss and Howe suggest that a Civic generational type forms when the leading edge of such a generation is approaching 30 years of age when the emergency erupts. In an earlier cycle the eldest peers of Alexander Hamilton's and Abigail Adams's Republican generation turned 31 in 1773 as the *HMS Gaspee* affair and the Boston Tea Party brought British-American relations to a fever pitch. More recently, the leading members of Ann Landers's and Billy Graham's GI generation turned 28 in 1929 as Wall Street crashed and the American Dream seemed in danger of ending in the first wintry winds of the Great Depression.

But the generational alignment was different when the crisis over slavery and states' rights within the Union boiled over in 1860 with the election of Lincoln and the secession of South Carolina. The oldest members of the Progressive generation following the Gilded generation of Nomads were only 17 in 1860—too young for much more than service as drummer boys and canteen fillers for both sides. The horrific casualties caused parents and civilian adults to ratchet up protection of children and youth to the point of suffocation.

After the War, Strauss and Howe observe:

> [N]o rising generation emerged to fulfill the usual **Civic** role of building public institutions to realize the **Transcendentals'** visions. Instead, the **Gilded** aged into a unique **Reactive-Civic** hybrid, and, in midlife, presided over a period of unusual cultural and spiritual staleness. Likewise, although the **Progressives** had been raised with a protective prewar nurture that prepared them to come of age as a **Civic** generation, they emerged from the Civil War scarred rather than ennobled. Acquiring little collective confidence as young adults, they left their future in the hands of the **Gilded** and developed a distinctly **Adaptive** peer personality.[2]

This scenario has direct bearing on our current situation. The September 11, 2001, terrorist attacks occurred as the newest generation of Americans slated to become Civics turned 19. Adults making life-and-death decisions can draw important lessons from the Civil War cycle: "how generational constellations can become dangerous, how types can play their life-cycle scripts too aggressively . . . that history is *not* predetermined, that the actions people take . . . can fundamentally alter the course of history."[3] Adult generations ahead of the Millennials can indulge their wishes for vengeance and war as the Civil War-era Transcendentalists and Gilded did, but such an indulgence could blight the prospects of this fledgling Civic generation. Self-control and patience by the Boomers and Xers will allow a few more critical years to pass, until the generational alignment turns to a point of somewhat less danger than replaying the Civil War generational cycle.

Youth

A Civic type of generation is being born at the beginning of a new century, even as this group's Civic grandparents were born at the turn of the last century. Such generations are born into periods of rekindled interest in children. Civic babies are celebrated and increasingly protected in infancy. Advancing neonatal medical care and this reawakened celebration of children caused medical insurance spending for premature Millennial infants to soar. In the early 1980s states began mandating infant safety seats in cars. Later in the decade a judge found a woman guilty of child endangerment because she had ingested illegal drugs while pregnant.[4] Pro-life activists encouraged adoption as an abortion alternative for pregnant teens. In the mid-1980s nervous Boomer parents watched the sensational McMartin trial, involving sex-abuse allegations in a day-care center, and wondered about their own child-care arrangements. (The McMartins—a grandmother, mother, son, and daughter—ran a day-care facility in California. In 1984 they were charged with multiple counts of abuse. At the end of a dramatic 28-month trial none of the accused were found guilty.[5])

Both parents take a deep interest in the care and raising of these celebrated children. Many Boomer mothers breast-fed babies whenever it was physically possible and socially acceptable, and used breast pumps when it was not. Boomer fathers remembered their own often emotionally distant fathers and vowed they would be different. Boomer dads *are* different—changing diapers, making formula, and wielding spoon, bib, and splat mat when babies switch to solid foods. Distrustful of corporations and additives they can't pronounce, parents of these kids are into natural and organic food. Organic baby food sales rose from $1.1 million to $25.1 million between 1989 and 1995.[6]

These parental actions echoed similar approaches taken by the Missionary generation of parents with their Civic generation of GI children in the early 20th century. Parents started administering newly available vitamins and daily spoonfuls of cod-liver oil for their children's health. The temperance movement against alcohol became militant, even violent, as Carry Nation attacked her first saloon with an ax in 1900. Minnesota was not alone in enacting a minimum labor age (14) for turn-of-the-century children.[7] States began adopting and enforcing school truancy laws. Parents added vitamins to food and supported anti-hookworm drugs. Schools added milk monitor programs to ensure a minimum daily intake of milk by every child.[8]

Values for Children

Boomers seek to equip their Millennial children to face an outer world that Boomers often see as anarchic or amoral. Boomers living by what might be called the 3 Vs—vision, values, and virtue—have laid down expectations of character and spiritual formation. The result of this insistence on virtue (formerly called morality) is a Millennial generation being raised on the new 3 Rs—rules, respect, responsibility. The 17th century Glorious generation grew up under a similar tutelage. Under the governance of their Puritan parents, Glorious children learned the correct relationship to all figures of authority from the Fifth Commandment, "Honor thy father and thy mother." They were taught to answer the question "Who are here meant by Father and Mother?" with the memorized statement, "All our superiors, whether in Family, School, Church and Common-wealth."[9]

Millennials, like other Civics before them, are being taught a no-nonsense code of morality, of definite rights and wrongs. Parents point to Nomad young adults (Generation Xers, or in an earlier cycle, the Liberty generation) as visible counterexamples of behavior and lifestyles to *avoid*. Adults inculcate values of teamwork and problem-solving that are reinforced by peer pressure (through 1990s youth soccer teams, or through 1910s Girl Scout troops). Young Civics get the message that they are powerful, capable, competent, and able to achieve great deeds together.

Congregational youth workers and adult religious instructors stress truth, virtue, and right behavior, pressing their young charges with the questions "What is a good choice here?" and "What would be a bad one?" The right answer is usually the one that means the greatest good for the many, while selfish ends are denounced. Young Civics conclude that sins (whether against people or against God) have real consequences. On the other hand, if they work hard and play by the rules, adults will praise them as good and reward them.

Idealist generations have a liking for things natural and are concerned about the environment—values they work hard to pass on to their children. Teddy Roosevelt's expansion of the National Park System met with strong approval from turn-of-the-20th-century Missionaries. Boomers have made recycling commonplace, and have touched off arguments across the country about urban sprawl, wetland restoration, and wilderness preservation.

In religious circles this environmental emphasis is taught to Civic generations as a part of the doctrine of creation. Idealist parents often find natural wonders and the wilderness itself spiritually sublime, *conveying* the holy. Their Civic children feel a spiritual wonder too, but increasingly tend to understand the creation *itself* as holy. Watching Disney's *The Lion King*, Millennials heard Mufasa teach his son that we are "all connected in the great circle of life, Simba." Millennials have begun constructing a theology of God centered on themes of the value of creation and order.

This latter, their desire for order, grows in conjunction with a certain liking for hierarchy. Parental insistence on respect, that children show deference to and obey teachers, coaches, and others in traditional authority roles, produces in Civics a liking for order and agreement over who is in charge and who is not. A European visitor to the United States in the 1850s remarked on the Progressive generation (before the Civil War turned them from a germinating Civic generation into an Adaptive one). "A hundred wills move at once simultaneously, with an accuracy that was really amazing."[10]

The focus on moralistic instruction, order, and rationality as strategies for facing an amoral and confusing world produces a left-brained generation of concrete and sequential thinkers and doers. These trends are reinforced by a school system that is undergoing renovation.

Schools

Schools take a visible turn for the better when Civics begin formal education. Teaching gains prestige, and educational standards for students are enforced. For the sake of their children, Boomers are rewriting state laws to allow easier transitions from other careers into teaching.

Earlier Civic generations have benefited from a similar improvement of schools and of their performance in them. In 1853 Massachusetts passed a law mandating school attendance for Progressive children up to age 10. Later in the 1850s the high school movement took hold across many states, founded on the idea that more than the 3 Rs would be needed in adults in the coming years.[11] Two centuries earlier the Puritans began requiring Glorious generation children to learn enough reading and vocabulary that they could read the Scriptures (which would give them a rich vocabulary indeed).

The focus in these reinvigorated schools moves away from emotional exploration, esteem-building, and individual creativity toward reasoning, problem solving, and teamwork. This emphasis toward group effort is linked to the rise of the school-uniform movement. Catholic parochial school students and elite, private-academy students have had school uniforms for decades, but in the mid-1980s this idea began spreading into public schools. The motivation was threefold.

First, Boomer parents, teachers, and school administrators were reacting to the well-publicized incidents in poor schools of Gen X children being mugged by bullies or gang members for their Air Jordans (an expensive brand of athletic shoe). Gang members and gang "wannabes" would wear distinctive colors so that each side could pick out the enemy at a glance. Schools' banning virtually all gang emblems, hats, sunglasses, and jewelry made choosing up sides for a confrontation harder, and other students in uniform didn't provide obvious targets. Second, school uniforms cut down on many of the style competitions and economic class distinctions within the student body. With the elimination of the clothes competition, groups and cliques had one less way of judging and putting down outsiders. Finally, advocates of uniforms contended that students in uniform learn better, and that uniforms instill group cooperation and solidarity.

Similar instincts of the Missionary generation of parents led them to foster a similar uniformity with the childhood GI generation. They seized on Lord Baden-Powell's founding of the Boy Scouts in England and brought the Scouting movement to America in 1910, forming troops and making uniforms for their sons. The Girls Scouts followed in 1912, while in rural America the 4-H movement fulfilled a similar function. These organizations reinforced an ethos of social cooperation, service, and respect. Mottoes and slogans such as "A Scout is trustworthy, loyal, helpful, friendly, courteous," and the 4-H's "hands, head, heart, and health" reflect an effort to instill public virtue and wholesome images.

College faculty are just starting to see the results of a celebrated generation raised this way, and it both delights and puzzles them. David Brooks, writing for *The Atlantic Monthly* in April 2001 ("The Organization Kid") visited his alma mater, Princeton University. Interviewing his Boomer peers on the faculty about the incoming class of Millennials, Brooks noted two common reactions: (1) "I can't get any of these kids to argue with me"—a situation utterly different from that at, say, Columbia University in 1968, and (2) "I can't get any of these kids to call me by my first name"— evidence that may signal a rebirth of personal respect and regard for status and authority, or reflect the stress of high adult expectations.

Rising Adulthood

Civic generations moving into rising adulthood have found a crisis erupting, the economy on the rocks, and a major social issue at the boiling point (independence, secession, the Depression, and a world war). Older adult generations (of Idealists and Nomads) are determined that their children should achieve the latest version of the American Dream. They make major personal and societal sacrifices on behalf of the Civics. Executives cut their own pay, and older workers take early leave from the labor force or are forced out to spare new workers the brunt of rising unemployment.

When these private-sector efforts prove inadequate (and they always have), governmental efforts and spending increase sharply. Franklin Roosevelt's Civilian Conservation Corps enrolled over a million GI generation men. Fed, clothed, and housed in military-like barracks, these uniformed, willing young men planted trees by the thousands to control erosion and built visitor facilities and hiking trails at hundreds of national and state parks. In an earlier period Congress passed the 1862 Homestead Act, giving clear title to 160 acres to anyone willing to work the land for five years. These efforts were construed not as welfare, but as programs and pilot projects that made for meaningful work and acquisition of skills, and that served as models for vast private and public efforts 10 or 20 years later.

Historically these public programs have focused on work for men because of the scarcity of jobs (even with all the private and governmental efforts). Women are often directed into traditional, home-centered roles. Women of these generations often see hearth and home as their place and child-rearing as their career. Like a congregation, home becomes a haven from the pressures of the social upheaval. The CCC and WPA (Works

Progress Administration) "boys" were encouraged to send nearly all their meager earnings home to parents or wives.

The habit of scrimping ignites a desire for middle-class status and the economic goods Civics are forced to do without for a long time (but which they often remember from their youth). These hard times lead to the success of products that are versatile and well made. Such quality is more easily achieved when product lines are few, focused, and standardized, and uniformity emerges as a pragmatic virtue. Scientists and engineers rise to new prestige among Civics. Appreciation for efficiency and application of scientific principles reinforces the earlier left-brain bias of this generation.

The social crises Civic generations have encountered in rising adulthood have usually been accompanied by a major war. Civic generations provide the armed forces with their soldiers, sailors, and (in the 20th century) air crews. They were the Minutemen, militia, and Continental soldiers whom Washington led through six long years of hardship to triumph. They were the Mutt and Jeff dogfaces of Anzio and Saipan and the "Rosie the Riveter" home-front factory hands, the Merchant Marine longshoremen, and, as General George Marshall of the Missionary generation called them, "The best damn kids in the world."[12]

With parent-age elders setting strategy and providing moral justification, and next-elder generation Nomads contributing canny fighting leadership and get-it-done civilian ingenuity, Civic generations face the crisis as team-playing, unified troops, both in and out of the military. And, with the important exception of the Civil War, it works: they win, so far.

Religion

With the outer world in upheaval, a corresponding yearning arises for the inner world to be calm. As Civics move through their rising adulthood, the times are seen as too harsh to allow indulgence in spiritual questing and innovation. Spiritual questions, denominational issues, and forms of worship all become more settled, or are put on automatic while real needs get met and solved.

Young adult Civics hear two emphases in the preaching from older generations. Graying Idealists in the pulpit tend to support the righteousness of America and the justice of its causes. Devoted Nomads call for pragmatic solutions applied to immediate social concerns. Listening to these two generations, Civics develop the idea that the solution to the social crisis combines righteousness and pragmatism in ways that reorder society—an insight they put to use when their turn to lead comes.

The emphasis of Nomad religious leaders on pragmatic solutions fosters a growing acceptance of the idea among Civics of church, synagogue, or mosque as a gathered community, offering mutual support, aid, and encouragement. A growing yearning for the joy and blessings of the faith sets in during such times. Partly this response is an escape from surrounding grimness, but partly it is sound, because all religions contain an element of hope, even joy, that burns more fiercely in times of trial. Such an emphasis serves as a corrective to the Idealist emphasis on sacrifice, judgmentalism, and even martyrdom.

Midlife

A grateful nation showers praise on returning veterans, rewards them with land grants, pensions, or preferences in education and hiring, and gives them the reins of power early. Indeed, Civic generations have had a pattern of coming to leadership early in life (in their late 30s or early 40s), and holding leadership for a long time.

In politics, Thomas Jefferson began a 24-year hold on the presidency by his Republican generation. In 200 years that group was outdone only by the GIs of the 20th century, beginning with the two-GI campaign of 1960 (Kennedy vs. Nixon). Not until 1992 did the GIs finally pass on the presidency to another generation—and then not to the next-in-line Silents, but rather to Boomer Bill Clinton, followed by Boomer George W. Bush.

In business in the early 2000s very few 39-year-olds are named CEO of an established corporation. But the board of directors of Bell and Howell, the leading technology company of the 1950s, named Charles Percy as CEO at age 39. Likewise, 39-year-old Lee Iacocca was handed the keys to the Ford Motor Division, and he promptly produced automotive history with the 1964 Mustang.

And how do Civics lead? They invent all sorts of things and strive to be modern, scientific, and rational (which they call being reasonable). Civic leadership in both secular and sacred circles is highly rational. Their leadership approach is left-brained, hierarchical, concrete, and sequential. At its best, this approach achieves a combination of harmony and balance that is admired far into the future. James Madison's checks-and-balances Constitution and Pierre L'Enfant's hub-and-spoke street pattern of buildings and park vistas that mark Washington, D.C., are distinctive products of Civic leadership.

Most notably, Civics build. More than any other generational type, Civic generations rework the physical face of America. They have built infrastructure: ports and post roads in the early 1700s; canals, railroads, and telegraph lines in the 1800s; and interstate highways and airports after World War II. They build houses and cities, often on a uniform pattern— the crisp, no-nonsense saltboxes of New England and the deep shaded porches of 1720 Charleston, or the repetitive suburban Levittowns of the 1950s.

Civic generations think big in tangible constructions, the opposite of their parents, who think big in abstract ideas and ideals. Jefferson doubled the size of the country with the Louisiana Purchase. President Madison hoped to annex Canada in the War of 1812.

Parenting and Schools

Civics in midlife have grown comfortable with men working in the larger world and women working at home. As Civics take over the lead in parenting, men typically pass off most of child-rearing to women at home. The new prosperity reinforces this separation as paychecks swell and the one-breadwinner middle class becomes standard.

Men hard at work outside the home increasingly emphasize rational left-brain functioning. Human feelings, with the exception of anger, are increasingly seen as womanly. Raising children increasingly becomes the work of Civic mothers. Many Awakeners later vowed with revivalist George Whitefield "to make good my mother's expectations" or chose with Samuel Adams to abandon worldly careers to please their mothers' "religious principles."[13]

Childbirth follows medical and scientific principles that are deemed the most modern for the era.[14] Those rearing children look for sensible principles, leading Dr. Benjamin Spock to wild popularity among GI parents in his 1946 book on child nurture, of letting children be children. Parents remembered their own childhoods of increasing regimentation, but with the broad peace now at hand, they reversed their own upbringing by loosening rules and allowing children to revel in the fresh prosperity through their play. Having seen a rather frenetic adult world in their youth from behind their childhood walls, and now emerging from a crisis in triumph, Civics felt that it was time to relax a bit.

Civic generations move parenting away from structure toward relaxation. Exceptions to rules and expectations, first for behavior, then for academic performance, increase as indulgence gains ground. The World War II GI generation followed this pattern with their Boomer children. Their indulgence became apparent beginning in 1960. Boomers taking the rather objective SAT college entrance exam began a much lamented 17-year decline in scores. But these same 17 years saw the number of college freshmen reporting a high school grade point of 4.0 (all As) triple.[15]

Children are increasingly indulged, while busy adults build, organize, and socialize with each other at home, in clubs, and in the congregation.

Religion

One of the places midlife Civics meet and relate to each other is in religious settings. Having been raised on an ethos of rules, respect, and responsibility, Civics take their religious obligations seriously. They set attendance records, make and fill annual pledges, and serve on committees. They also continue and intensify the interchurch and interreligious cooperation they saw modeled in their generation's recent crisis.

First, they join and attend regularly in great numbers. The GIs made mainline churches the *mainline* in the 1950s. "In 1958 [church membership] was 109,557,741, or about 63 percent, marking an all-time high in the nation's history."[16] (Older congregational members and retired clergy who long for the good old days remember correctly the enormous throngs of these years. They often misunderstand how much of an anomaly this decade was.)

Second, Civics in midlife emphasize structures larger than the congregation. As George Washington was sworn in as president in 1789, the Methodists established a "book concern," the first denominational publishing arm. In the early 1700s the Presbyterians of the Glorious generation formed both presbyteries and synods beyond the congregational level.[17] (Incidentally, the Presbyterians may well be a denomination Civics can really enjoy. In their governing documents since the 1700s the Presbyterian catchphrase has been "Let all things be done decently and in order.")

Third, Civics emphasize points of commonality between their own faith and the faith of others, under the rubric, "We all really want the same thing"—often true for Civics, but a mystery to other generations. Republican generation Congregationalists and Presbyterians formed a joint mission board for sending missionaries to the Oregon Territory after the War of 1812. The GIs were instrumental in forming the National Council of Churches in 1950 and, in 1962, the Consultation on Christian Union (COCU), first an organic union effort; later a theological dialogue of nine Protestant bodies aimed at "full communion." (A recent name change christened it "Churches Uniting in Christ" [CUIC].)

Fourth, American civil religion gets a boost as denominational differences are downplayed. While sociologist Robert Bellah was the first to publish the term "American civil religion" in 1967, the concept behind it goes much further back. Already in the 1830s Rabbi Isaac Wise was working among American Jews with an idea toward Americanizing Judaism, shorn of its outworn empty rites, and made more modern and understandable— qualities dear to Civics. The movement culminated with the Pittsburgh Declaration of 1885 establishing Reform Judaism.

Fifth, the downplaying of differences often stems from a reaction by adult Civics to what they remember of their parents' passion and religion of the heart. "As children [members of the Glorious generation] looked upon the passion and poverty of their parents as an embarrassment to be transcended."[18] This reaction frequently leads to an overemphasis on what might be called a "head faith." The Civics' embrace of reason and logic, and their apparent success in applying both in solving all sorts of secular problems often leads them to prefer human rationalism over revealed religious doctrine. Republicans like Jefferson touted Deism, hoping it would become the religion of the land. Jefferson believed common human principles and reason would serve as a better basis for national unity than competing claims of revealed religion. He tried to help his cause by publishing a Bible in 1816, carefully editing out all the irrational or passionate elements (like miracles) and the portions that would support revealed religion (like Mount Sinai or the Damascus Road).

Finally, just as the generation is doing in the secular world, Civics enjoy building temples and putting on additions. The high value they place on fitting in, getting along, and downplaying differences leads to a uniformity in their religious buildings. Most readers can look around their communities and see the effects of the 1940s postwar building boom. Brick walls cover concrete-block support walls. Religious education wings are of brick, fitted with aluminum-frame windows, even when the main structure is a stone Gothic or a steepled white clapboard building. (These same materials and rectangular proportions were used to build shopping centers, city halls, fire stations, and consolidated elementary schools.)

Religious Leadership

Moving into midlife, Civics lead differently from other generations. Their style and assumptions are distinctive. Consider first a list of religious figures who were members of a Civic generation. (This list is rather shorter than for the other types, since the Civil War cycle did not produce a Civic type.)

TABLE OF CIVIC RELIGIOUS NOTABLES

Years	Name	Contribution
1656–1730	Thomas Bray	Anglican founder of Society for the Propagation of the Gospel (1701) to promote Anglicanism as a unifying power across all colonies. Successful in spreading the Anglican (later Episcopal) Church beyond its Chesapeake Bay base.
1745–1801	Jonathan Edwards the Younger	New England Congregationalist defender of Trinitarianism vs. rising Unitarians.
1748–1836	William White	Episcopal priest, ardent patriot. Chaplain of Continental Congress 1777–1789. Father of Protestant Episcopal Church in wreckage of Anglicanism after Revolution.
1751–1820	Judith Sergeant	A lonely female voice in a Civic generation, noted Murray for her 1790 essay "The Equality of the Sexes."

1751–1797	Elhanan Winchester	Prominent Baptist minister who, at end of 1780s, became a Universalist pastor.
1752–1817	Timothy Dwight	New England Congregationalist and defender of Trinitarianism. Elected President of Yale University in 1795 at age 43.
1764–1806	Elihu Palmer	In 1794 organized the Deistical Society of New York City to promote Deism and dispute revealed religion.
1904–1967 1906–1964	John Courtney Murray and Gustave Weigel	Both Roman Catholic, joint authors, *We Hold These Truths* (1960), arguing that political democracy, including separation of church and state, could be grounded on Catholic, and more important, Christian principles.[19]
1905–	Margaret Kuhn	Presbyterian lay church worker and long-time volunteer for the YWCA. Founder of Gray Panthers in 1970, a leading group to improve the status of seniors. Author, *Get Out There and Do Something about Aging* (1972).
1907–1972	Abraham Heschel	Towering rabbinic theologian of 20th century, prolific author of over 40 books. *The Sabbath* (1951), *Quest for God* (1954), *God in Search of Man* (1955).
1917–	Theodore Hesburgh	Roman Catholic priest, named president of NotreDame in 1952 at age 35, and led the university to national academic prominence. Also served on the National Science Board and the U.S. Civil Rights Commission.
1918–	Billy Graham	Southern Baptist minister and evangelist, noted for his mass rallies, use of television, and, in his earlier years, his identification of Americanism with Christianity.

1918–	Oral Roberts	Pentecostal preacher and faith healer. Pioneer in use of television among evangelicals. Founder of Oral Roberts University.
1920–	Robert Drinan	Roman Catholic priest, law professor, and member of Congress. Named dean of Boston Law College at age 36.
1921–	William (Bill) Bright	Texas businessman, founder of Campus Crusade for Christ and InterVarsity Press. American revivalism condensed to "Four Spiritual Laws" pamphlet that marked college campuses for decades.

Themes that emerge in studying prior Civic generations (and which may emerge in the current Millennial generation) are attitudes of cooperation and community. Not founders of sects or new religions, they are the great preservers and strengtheners of established faiths. They like harmony, balance, and logic, and value clarity over style. Order and reason are considered virtues, while spiritual passion and religious innovation are suspect.

Civic generations are raised from childhood to take responsibility and to place a high value on joining and contributing to organizations. They have repeatedly displayed an ordering, stabilizing trait. Civic generations are comfortable with hierarchy—a trait that makes other generations cringe or laugh, but which they find reassuring. Some are in charge—and everyone else salutes and works together. By following established norms, Civics both honor the past and connect with each other in the present.

Presented with our fill-in-the-blank sentence, "God is _____," Civic generations would modify the statement by making it read "*Our* God is_____." Their values of teamwork, cooperation, and community assert themselves. (After all, when GI notable Charles Lindbergh wrote his autobiography—by definition an individualistic work—he titled it *We*.) Civics would complete the statement to read, "Our God is *almighty*." Having been raised on a can-do ethos of accomplishment, and propelled by success in their rising adulthood in mastering a secular crisis, Civics launch into leadership imitating a God who creates and orders the universe.

David serves as a biblical role model for Civics. Anointed as a youth to be king, David slew Goliath and became a hero to Israel. He was submissive to the Lord's anointed, Saul, showing respect for hierarchy. Even when Saul drove him out, David did not revolt against him or kill him when he had the chance. When Saul died, David succeeded in winning the war against the Philistines. As he moved into midlife, David's generation gained peace and prosperity, built cities and temples, and unified Israel's tribes into a nation by centering religious and state power in Jerusalem.

David's reign was marred by the Bathsheba scandal, and in consequence he was barred from fulfilling his passion to build a Temple in Jerusalem. He was left shaken and saddened by the fury of a revolt led by his son Absalom. He died in his palace, surrounded by family and all he had built for God. To this day Jews call David their greatest king, whose six-pointed star serves as a symbol of their faith.

Communication

As communicators and preachers, Civics are logical and well organized, if somewhat formulaic. They may use their seminary training deep into their clergy careers by preaching three points and a poem. The three points will be sequential and fit together in a logical fashion, while the poem (sometimes the stanza of a hymn) will both summarize the sermon theme and serve as a right-brain balance to the left-brain main body. Themes related to community and the people of God figure prominently. Clergy typically preach about a lofty God of great power and creativity and a rational God of order and logic—far different from their parents' mystical, immanent and passionate God.

Civic preachers might interpret the Parable of the Good Samaritan along these lines:

The man going down to Jericho makes the mistake of traveling alone, and he pays for it. But when the Samaritan comes along, he does what any good, logical, normal person would do—he helps.

First, the Samaritan patches up the victim with oil, wine, and bandages—which is as good as medicine was in those days. Second, he sees he can't leave the man on the ground, so he loads him on his donkey to take him out of trouble. Third, when they get to the inn, the Samaritan pays the innkeeper and puts him in charge of caring for this victim. If the innkeeper wants to pay someone to nurse the man, or to pay for a doctor, or even to pay someone to take a message to the victim's family—it's up to the innkeeper.

This is how Jesus wanted his church to be, everyone connected to each other and everyone showing God's power by caring for each other.

Pastoral counseling can be a particular challenge. Civic men in particular are uncomfortable with rummaging about in emotional attics. They prefer shorter, to-the-point conversations and sessions. Admiring expertise, they are quite willing to refer parishioners to psychologists, psychiatrists, and other experts in the field. People who are yearning for spiritual excitement or enthusiasm often remind Civics of their parents, a factor that can get in the way of effective counseling and guidance.

On the other hand, when they can analyze a given problem, these clergy can be helpful. Their rationality often gives them an important counseling distance that lets them say with the GI generation's Ann Landers: "Wake up and smell the coffee." Having brought a counseling session to such a wake-up moment, they are also good at coming up with practical, day-to-day solutions.

Often such solutions involve doing something—saying three Hail Marys, or making an apology, or visiting a mental health expert. Such changing behaviors can bring a corresponding change in outlook. But all this activity has a downside too. The Civics' propensity for *doing* leaves them with a weakness for works-righteousness. They can take St. Paul's admonition of "work out your own salvation" too much to heart. It is this charge of empty activity that forms the basis for the strongest critique Civics face in their lives—the uproar of their own children. This roar erupts just as the leading edge of Civic generations begins entering elderhood.

Elderhood

As people at the leading edge of a Civic generation begin entering elderhood, they encounter a generation that doesn't adore them: their own Idealist children. Civics up to now have found older Idealists cherishing them and younger Adaptives awed by them. But when their own children begin coming of age, history has shown a regular pattern of youthful fury directed at parents. The Puritans, Awakeners, Transcendentals, Missionaries, and

Boomers each erupted against emotionally distant fathers and faith practices that struck the younger generation as too much duty and not enough zeal. Tradition is scorned and vision is demanded, something Civics are not good at. George Bush the elder confessed in the 1992 primaries that he (and his generation) had trouble with "the vision thing."

After some years of battling across the generation gap (with nimble-footed Adaptives in the crossfire), some sort of social truce is reached. Civics stay personally busy and politically potent since they still do things together so well. The GIs flooded the membership ranks of the AARP, made Medicare and Medicaid the first-ever publicly funded senior medical plans, and added cost-of-living escalators to Social Security payments. They were still more comfortable with their peers than with other generations, so families watched GIs move away to the Sunbelt—often central Florida or Arizona.

Financially, Civic generations reach elderhood in a rather comfortable state. Proceeds from the sale of the home acquired from downsizing and moving into a cheaper townhouse in a retirement community often provided a comfortable nest egg for many GIs. (In 1958 the national average price for a new home was about $15,000. The mortgage payment typically ran $100 a month for 20 years. The same 1250-square-foot suburban house, fully paid for in the mid 1970s, would fetch $100,000.[20] The financial payoff for GIs was substantial.)

Stewardship

Religious leaders designing stewardship efforts will still find many of this generation connected to their congregations. GIs currently live in three primary settings:

- In retirement communities with their peers. Civics often move out of state, either temporarily for the winter months, or more permanently. While they associate (formally or informally) with their winter congregation, they will still feel a strong sense of loyalty and belonging to their base congregation.
- In nursing homes or assisted-living facilities around the community. With their oldest members passing 100, many GIs find their health deteriorating and are forced to give up their homes. For such a bustling generation, this step comes hard and is often depressing or frustrating.

- In the 800–1,200 square foot, cookie-cutter tract house that they bought new between 1946 and 1960. Many times a GI generation widow continues to keep house where all the memories live and where she can stay connected with her friends at church and the Legion hall.

Financially, Social Security has been a great deal for GIs. The total contribution they and their employers made to Social Security during all their working years was completely paid back to them within three years of retirement. Since then they have been collecting from everyone else. (This is a fact they generally would like to deny, and they may become upset when challenged about it.) They worry about health-care costs and provided some of the force behind the 2000 presidential campaign arguments over publicly-funded prescription drug benefits. They look carefully at every disbursement of their funds.

The Stewardship Request

Congregational leaders approaching members of the GI generation can be more effective if they take into account some of this generation's assumptions. When researcher George Barna studied the senior generation in the early 1990s (not taking into account Strauss and Howe's boundaries, he reported: "Seniors (i.e., those born 1926 or earlier) are much more likely than any other group to describe themselves as religious; feel absolutely committed to the Christian faith; reject the notion that Jesus Christ sinned during His time on earth; describe God in orthodox, Biblical terms; and disagree strongly that the Bible teaches that money is the root of all evil."[21]

- GIs have a taste for hierarchy and have lived with sharp gender distinctions. A male caller for the stewardship or capital funds drive may be more effective with GIs (for men are seen as more in charge). A significant exception is a situation in which the top clergy leader in a congregation is a woman: her title trumps her gender, especially in the eyes of GI generation women. As long as the woman leader comes across as decisive, warm, and cheery, she will get a good response.
- GIs deeply appreciate hosting a stewardship caller in the home, face to face. They will often want to talk about past triumphs and monetary sacrifices they have made, and they expect to be listened to.

- GIs often expect a certain formality (Mr. Anderson/ Mrs. Larson/ Miss Hansen—and Ms. is generally not used). Only when you are invited to be informal ("Oh, call me Helga, please!"), should first names be used. If such an invitation never comes, then be formal. GIs will perceive this practice as deferential and polite. They like this courtesy and expect it from those younger than themselves (which these days is almost everybody).

- Dressing conservatively shows seriousness and propriety. GIs think men with a three-day stubble of beard are irresponsible. They think bodies should be pierced only to accommodate earrings (one per ear) to be worn only by women. They hold these standards for everyone, not just for themselves.

- Express appreciation for the GIs' legacy—the property and facilities they have provided. They often feel that younger generations take their contributions (especially physical ones) for granted, so such appreciation can lessen their sense of being overlooked.

- Express repeated gratitude for past support and loyalty to the congregation's life and traditions. Stress the tradition of giving that has sustained the congregation through good times and bad. Denominational and institutional loyalty are high values and should be stressed.

- GIs often find themselves asked for money, but *not* for input, ideas, or problem-solving, so asking for such input on some issue in the congregation can be helpful. (The ideas GIs offer when asked to solve a problem may well remind Boomer-age callers of their parents' approach to life and problems. Such Boomer callers should anticipate their own reactions to such ideas ahead of time.)

- Be willing to get to the bottom line. It is helpful to emphasize the big picture of the congregation in concrete terms, particularly *numbers* (attendance, square feet added or remodeled, for example) for this left-brained, sequential-thinking generation.

- Mention congregational financial successes: debt reduction, mortgage payoffs or refinancings, and contributions and support for the larger denomination, disaster relief, or rebuilding efforts. Such successes show responsibility, care with money, denominational loyalty, and cooperation by God's people to lend a hand after a disaster.

- Express your own dedication to the congregation. A Generation X caller, or someone new to the congregation, might say something like, "The reason I'm on the stewardship team this year is that I want First

Church to be a home for me and my family—a place where we can really settle and put down roots."

Death and Legacy

Congregations and religious groups can take some steps to minister to this generation of aging doers. Agencies that care for elders can arrange for traditional, denominational worship services to be held in retirement communities. If a chapel can be reset easily with symbols of Catholic, Protestant, or Jewish traditions, Civics will appreciate the thoughtfulness.

Being useful and active matters a great deal to this generation. One retirement home in Toledo, Ohio, found a way to harness this urge. They designed a large kitchen to allow GI generation women to continue baking and cooking from wheelchairs and walkers. Staff people would do some of the heavy lifting and lend a hand in getting things into and out of the oven, but the accumulated and delicious wisdom of decades made for great daily desserts in the dining room. In a similar way, the home set up a full-scale woodworking shop, arranged for wheelchairs and walkers. Staff members here would provide the extra pair of hands on many maneuvers. The output from the shop resulted in chair rails and handrails along the halls and in the rooms, crown moldings, bookcases, magazine racks, and plant stands both on the site and for sale to the public. In both the seniors' kitchen and the workshop, classes were offered for all ranges of ability, sometimes taught by the seniors themselves, at other times by outsiders.

GI generation members grew up showing respect and deference to their elders. As they have gotten old, they have expected to be on the receiving end of such treatment, but often they have not received it. Such respect and deference is something faith communities can purposefully give their seniors. Listening to them, treating them with honor and respect, and using titles (Mrs. or Dr.) are little things that will be cherished by this generation.

Middle-aged Americans shocked by the World Trade Center attacks rallied around one another, offering help, comfort, and money. They tried to explain what the terrorist acts meant to the Millennial generation of children. GI generation members were asked for their memories of what it was like to be surprised and attacked as a nation. Many GIs nodded sagely, recounting Pearl Harbor and the years before and after when they saw a nation bound together. Only rarely are GIs asked for such memories, and religious communities might seek such accounts more purposefully.

Like all other generations, Civics face their own mortality in their own way. Seeing their outer-world accomplishments neglected or even depreciated often depresses them. (Jefferson doubted that the nation he worked so hard to bring to life would survive the passing of his Republican generation.) Civics' faith is not always a comfort at this point. Elders often keep traditions alive as an outward exercise of good works rather than because they find inner comfort, faith, and hope in these works. Doctrines of heaven or resurrection have a mystical quality that seems to defy logic, so they are often hard for Civics to embrace. Funerals of veterans are often marked more with emblems of military service and civil religion than with denominational symbols.

Civics can leave substantial estates for their heirs, although these are overwhelmingly on a middle-class scale (rather than a Rockefeller-like fortune). In recent times these estates have often been more depleted than heirs expected by long-term health-care costs.

Civics leave a legacy of optimism, hope, and community. Tireless builders and careful organizers, these dutiful heirs of King David show other generations how dreams and hopes become reality.

GENERATIONAL TURNINGS

Each generation is defined by a common persona or type shared by all the people born in a range of years. The order of the generational types is fixed (Idealist, Nomad, Civic, Adaptive; but the Civil War cycle was an exception, omitting the Civic type.) The generational types pass through the four stages of life in a repeating cycle, like water from a faucet flowing through the compartments of an ice cube tray. Now usually the generations are straddling two life stages (midlife and elderhood, for example). But in certain years each of the four generations fairly fills one stage of life. Strauss and Howe call each of these four points when the generations are aligned the beginning of a Turning. Such a Turning lasts until the final members of a given generation move into the next life stage (about 22 years later).

During the years of a Turning, American society and its institutions display a distinctive character. In particular, when leadership is the prime task in society, institutions, corporations, and congregations, the traits of the generation in midlife make a vast difference in these institutions' responses to events. Chapters 9 through 12 examine the interactions *between* generations in each Turning and discuss how these relationships affect faith communities.

Strauss and Howe label the Turnings this way:

First Turning	**A High**:
	Civics moving into Midlife
Second Turning	**An Awakening**:
	Adaptives moving into Midlife
Third Turning	**An Unraveling:**
	Idealists moving into Midlife
Fourth Turning	**A Crisis:**
	Nomads moving into Midlife

CHAPTER 9

IF YOU BUILD IT,
WE'LL ALL COME

Strauss and Howe identify the following sets of dates as periods of a First
Turning, which they designate as a High.

FIRST TURNING—A HIGH

1946-1964
1865-1886
1794-1822
1704-1727

At the beginning of a First Turning, the four generational types have
just come into the alignment shown on the left side of chart below. Through
the coming 20 to 25 years or so, the four types gradually move up one life
stage to the alignment shown on the right. The generation whose members
are in elderhood at the beginning of a Turning die, with only a few scattered
long-lived seniors surviving to the end of the Turning. But the same
generational type re-emerges in the births of a new generation that fills the
youth stage of life by the end of the Turning.

FIRST TURNING GENERATIONAL ALIGNMENT

Stage of Life	Beginning of Turning	End of Turning
Elderhood	Idealists	Nomad
Midlife	Nomad	Civic
Rising Adulthood	Civic	Adaptive
Youth	Adaptive	New Idealist

<<<<<18 to 25 years>>>>>

The Lord God took the man and put him in the Garden of
Eden to till it and keep it.

—Genesis 2:15

A First Turning begins with the end of a crisis. After years of hurting, worry, fear, and fighting, a new dawn breaks across the country. A crisis has been met and mastered, and we have come out the other side—unified, triumphant, and ready to embrace a peaceful and sunny future that has come into the present. The Civics, having overcome a crisis, begin to move out of rising adulthood into midlife and leadership.

Looking at Strauss and Howe's beginning dates of these eras, readers will recognize the end of World War II in 1945 as a historic watershed. Marking the end of the Civil War era, 1865 also saw the beginning of an industrial revolution in the North, expansion along the frontier, and Reconstruction in the South. In 1794 the American Revolutionary War era and its chaotic aftermath were brought to an orderly settlement with the adoption of the Constitution, the inauguration of George Washington, and the establishment of a stable economy under Alexander Hamilton. The year 1704 closed a period of Colonial wars, both internal and against coalitions of New Spain, New France, and Native American tribes.

The Economy

People at the beginning of a First Turning have a great desire for peace, and the things of peace. As the Civil War song put it:

. . . O The men will cheer, the boys will shout

The ladies, they will all turn out

And we'll all feel gay, When Johnny comes marching home.[1]

Returning veterans spread out across the land to their homes, shops, farms, towns, offices, ranches, and mines. They encounter others of their generation who, though not having served on the front lines, also experienced a certain regimented discipline in supporting the war effort and keeping the home fires burning. In all cases but one (the Civil War) the generation that forged and fired the cannons has been the Civics. Having scrimped and denied themselves through the crisis, they now turn their teamwork ethos and success-fueled optimism into making the things of peace. "The Great American Boom is on," crowed *Fortune* magazine in 1946, "and there's no measuring it. The old yardsticks just won't do."[2] Sixty million members of the GI generation beat their swords into plowshares and launched the post–World War II expansion. Walt Whitman described the postwar exuberance after the end of the Civil War: "Open up all your valves and let her go—swing, whirl with the rest—you will soon get under such momentum you can't stop if you would."[3]

In a First Turning, a powerful coalition of governmental bodies, business interests, and a willing work force builds a massive infrastructure for moving information and goods. Such a coalition delivered goods, services, and information to the military for years in the Fourth Turning. Now it does the same for civilians.

The early 1700s Glorious generation built cities (New Orleans, Charleston) and established seaports. The Republican generation of the 1790s dug a network of canals, traced roads across the Alleghenies, and provided a system of postal riders. Its members built ferries, bridges, and river ports (Pittsburgh, Cincinnati, St. Louis) that handled the increasing steam-powered riverboat traffic.

The post-Civil War Gilded generation, warping into a unique Civic-Nomad hybrid,[4] completed a transcontinental railroad network, and built iron bridges across large bodies of water (for instance, the Brooklyn Bridge, connecting Manhattan to Brooklyn). They dug and installed water mains under Manhattan that are still the primary source of fresh water for 18 million New Yorkers. They paved city streets, strung telegraph lines across the Plains, and erected grain elevators in every rural crossroads village through which a rail line ran.

The GIs listened as the Lost generation's Dwight Eisenhower recounted a cross-country road trip he had taken in 1919. The army convoy had taken 62 days to travel coast to coast.[4] Eisenhower thought America could do better, and the GIs agreed. During Eisenhower's tenure as president, 42,000 miles of interstate national defense highways, each one numbered and emblazoned with a red-white-and-blue shield marker, began to appear across America. Gas stations blossomed at every exit. In 1952 Kemmons Wilson began planting a national chain of standardized Holiday Inns that featured sparkling rooms, new mattresses, air conditioning, and a free reservation system. In 1955 Ray Kroc bought out the owners of a successful quick-service hamburger stand in southern California and began feeding the masses of auto travelers from his growing string of identical McDonald's restaurants, with a short, standardized menu that could be counted on to be safe and consistent.

Civics place a high value on fitting in and getting along with their community. This desire extends to a uniformity in their buildings. GIs built hospitals, airports, and suburban housing tracts, all using common plans and designed on similar scales. The houses looked alike. Businesses looked like schools, which often looked like city halls, which looked like businesses—and all of this was just fine with the GIs.

Institutional leadership

At the beginning of the Turning, midlife Nomad leaders seek to calm the national mood, take responsibility for hard choices, protect what has just been won, and preside over prosperity. The elderly Idealists, dying in increasing numbers, are pleased that *their* dreams are being realized before their aging eyes. The last of the Puritans died at the end of the 1600s, gratified that their rights as Englishmen, and the rights of younger generations, had been secured. Independence and a prosperous republic satisfied Benjamin Franklin's Awakeners at the end of the 18th century.

These canny, just-do-it Nomads provide pragmatic, innovative leadership. Through the hard years of the Fourth Turning, now coming to an end, they have tested and refined a welter of new ideas in technology, economic organization, inventions, and social organizations, all filtered through their question "What works best?" As the First Turning arrives, their solutions become the how-to manual for the do-things-by-the-book, up-and-coming Civics. The Civics edging into midlife leadership find notes, blueprints, and tested guidelines for their energy and optimism.

Nomad leadership is blunt, hard headed, and realistic, with an emphasis on results. Harry Truman met with the Soviet Ambassador in the closing days of World War II as Stalin was grabbing control of Eastern Europe with impunity. Truman said afterward, "I gave it to him straight, the old one-two." The Ambassador gasped during the conversation, "I have never been talked to like that in my life!" Truman shot back, "Live up to your agreements and you won't get talked to like that."[6]

Nomads in leadership also show their generation's propensity for protecting those younger than themselves. Nomad U.S. presidents have taken this task to include protecting the entire country. Truman authorized the building of the hydrogen bomb and the establishment of the Central Intelligence Agency. The Liberty generation's Washington and Adams persuaded Congress to build six state-of-the-art 42-gun frigates to protect the American coast. (One of these was the *USS Constitution*, still commissioned and at anchor in Boston harbor.)

The up-and-coming Civics fuse the dreams of the aging Idealists, the workable solutions of the next-elder Nomads who are relinquishing leadership, and their own team-playing ethos to make America and its institutions hum. The new rising adults, the often awestruck and sensitive Adaptives, apply their newly minted expertise to helping the bustling Civics untangle problems and soothe any hard feelings the Civics' hustling can leave in its wake. The whole culture feels relaxed, ready for fun, and confident that those running things know what they're doing.

First Turnings are eras of establishing institutions. Civics have a taste for order, balance, and clarity, and they work hard to regularize and organize their world. The James Madison Republicans established the U.S. Post Office in 1789, took the first census in 1790, and began circulating a national currency. New York Governor Dewitt Clinton cleared great stretches of Manhattan Island to impose a massive grid pattern of north-south avenues and numbered cross streets.

The post-Civil War Gilded Congress of 1866 adopted the metric system as the official U.S. system of weights and measures. In 1883 the entire country's local timekeeping was regularized into four time zones, allowing for more efficient scheduling of passenger trains, as well as the freight trains loading grain from the soon-familiar elevators that sprouted near the depots. In the east, leaders in Philadelphia, Boston, and New York demolished street after street of older wooden houses, replacing them with brownstone row houses, all with common roofs and matching stoops whose steps led down to the newly bricked sidewalks.

Parenting

Civic parents tending to their well-ordered outer world think they may have been rather overregimented in childhood. They remember how their own overprotected Third Turning childhoods led to a smothering approach to child-raising in the Fourth Turning just ended. In this Turning, a reaction sets in and Civics opt for a different approach. They encourage their children to look inward, explore their individuality, and express themselves freely.

The early 18th century Glorious generation took Cotton Mather's *The Well Ordered Family* to heart, raising children with material advantages that they themselves would have counted as luxuries.[7] The post-Civil War Gildeds followed Jacob Abbott's advice in his book *Gentle Measures in the Management of the Young*, "Children are generally not indulged enough." (Missionary Jane Addams would later scorn this happy childhood of her peers with the comment, "We were sickened with advantages."[8])

The other parenting generation in a First Turning, the younger Adaptives, remember their often stark, constrained childhoods. They gladly join older Civic parents in expanding possibilities for children, and in reinforcing Civic parents' tendencies toward indulging children. The Silent generation Adaptives of the 1950s and early 1960s resembled Rob Petrie on "The Dick Van Dyke Show," coming home to his son's incessant question, "Daddy, what did you bring me today?" Rob always had something in his pocket for little Ritchie.

Religion

During a First Turning, what is happening in the various faiths and denominations? What is worship like? How do religious leaders run congregations?

In a First Turning, denominational loyalty peaks, because institutional loyalty is an expression of team playing and community for the prominent Civics. Consequently the number of interfaith marriages is low. Likewise divorces and one-parent homes are unusual, since these are signs of disloyalty to the institution of marriage.

Religious bodies that are perceived as the mainstream in a Turning become powerful. The early 18th century Glorious legally established the Anglican Church in Virginia and the Carolinas and barred members of other denominations from political office. The Republican generation of John Adams's day responded in great numbers to the circuit-riding evangelists along the western frontier—in those days Ohio, Kentucky, and Alabama—and made the Methodists and Presbyterians the pacesetting denominations.

As in the secular realm, religious bodies in a First Turning embark on a period of constituting themselves. In 1707 the Baptists of Philadelphia first formed an association of congregations. In the next First Turning the Dutch Reformed Church broke ties with the mother church in Holland to become an independently constituted body in 1792.

While denominational loyalty is high, actual public differences between faiths are downplayed, and historic differences are no longer sources of controversy or division. Philadelphia in 1790 saw the founding convention of American Unitarians, who sought to end denominational quarreling by simplifying the "one in three, three in one" language of historic Trinitarian Christianity. Post-World War II GIs nodded in agreement as Lost generation President Dwight Eisenhower declared, "Our government makes no sense unless it is founded in a deeply felt religious faith—and I don't care what it is."[9] Their own GI generation Catholic, John F. Kennedy, reassured Protestant ministers in Houston in 1960 that he would make presidential decisions "without regard to outside religious pressure or dictate."[10]

Worship

In a First Turning, the Nomad worship leaders become the new denominational stalwarts. Having overcome their youthful skepticism, they embrace denominational norms for worship. As the Turning wears on, the Civic generation moves into worship leadership, and they continue these traditions as an expression of their respect for the past.

All generations tend to be satisfied with worship in a First Turning. Aging Nomads passing on the traditions see them carried out with style. Civic followers and congregation members cheerfully go along with their leaders. The rising adult Adaptives may chafe at the lack of choices and the sameness, but their deferential character and desire to be helpful dominates. The new Idealist youth are going along with Mom and Dad and spend much time in classrooms and newly built youth rooms.

Implications for Religious Bodies

The cycle of four generations passing through four Turnings repeats after a 90-95 year period. Knowing the impact Turnings have on religious bodies allows these leaders to prepare for the changes.

In a First Turning, as the new crop of Civics and the rising wave of Adaptives move into the nation's pulpits, the building boom is on.

Congregations and denominations plant new congregations, erect additions, and refurbish and remodel their facilities. Judicatory officials visit local congregations with blueprints, lot plans and denominational loan packages to undergird and extend the boom. (In a First Turning in 1698 the Glorious generation of Civics put up Trinity Church in Delaware, the oldest Protestant worship center in America still in continuous use.)

Congregations and religious institutions in a First Turning are usually run by a small body of leaders—historically they have often been exclusively male. Whether ordained or lay leaders, Civics are comfortable with hierarchy, and establish clear lines of authority and accountability. Their leadership style is planned and orderly, with appropriate follow-through. They are excellent builders of community, to which they believe everyone (especially others like themselves) can and wants to belong.

The aging Idealists have usually set overall goals for institutions, and these energetic Civic leaders focus on the how-tos of fulfilling these goals. These often-young Civic leaders look to the next elder Nomads for input about what is practical and workable. They look within themselves for energy, coordination, and achievement. Republican generation member Francis Asbury, one of the first Methodist bishops, was a tireless horseman and exemplified the idea of circuit-riding ministers in America. The freshly organized (1784) Methodists adopted Asbury's methods for tending to the new congregations between the Appalachians and the Mississippi.

The rising adult Adaptive religious leaders are commonly directed into youth work with their own late-wave peers and the coming crop of Idealist children. In doing ministry with these often-indulged youth, Adaptives gain practical experience with and insights into a very different generation. These Adaptives are often able to maintain a relationship with some of the young generation when the Second Turning arrives.

For the remainder of the First Turning, perhaps the most effective staff combination is a Civic-Adaptive one in multiple-staff congregations. A "dynamic duo" combination of midlife Civic and rising adult Adaptive covers the rational and emotional bases in a congregation. Rationality, decisiveness, and collaborative achievement are paired with emotional sensitivity, an ability to smooth ruffled feathers, and personal warmth. If good communication and goodwill prevail, such congregations will be places of tradition, growth, and comfort for both longtime and newer members.

The intergenerational dynamics of a First Turning are harmonious, with all generations finding reasons for cooperation. First Turnings are fondly remembered by those who live in them as a sort of Golden Age, filled with unity, purpose, prosperity, and peace. This golden age comes to an end in a Second Turning, because each generational type moves into a new stage of life. We will explore these different and far more strained dynamics in the next chapter.

ON THE OTHER HAND

Strauss and Howe use a traditional term as their designation for a Second Turning—an "Awakening." Historians have noted at least three American awakenings, periods when spiritual and religious issues have come to the forefront of society. The change from the outer-world focus of a First Turning to the inner-world focus of a Second Turning is quite sharp, and social unrest has usually broken out.

SECOND TURNING—AN AWAKENING

1964-1984
1886-1908
1822-1844
1727-1746
1621-1649

SECOND TURNING GENERATIONAL ALIGNMENT

Stage of Life	Beginning of Turning	End of Turning
Elderhood	Nomad ⟶	Civic
Midlife	Civic ⟶	Adaptive
Rising Adulthood	Adaptive ⟶	Idealist
Youth	Idealist	New Nomad

<<<<<18 to 25 years>>>>>

What do we want? Freedom! When do we want it? Now!

—Civil rights movement marching chant

At the beginning of a Second Turning, factories, schools, congregations, and government all hum with activity. Jobs are plentiful and well paying. Line workers produce quantities of products, which consumers will soon buy. Religious leaders preside over building programs and lead worship in keeping with tradition. Political leaders authorize digging canal systems, or preparing to send a man to the moon. Civic generation leaders in midlife see no reason this happy life of ever-growing prosperity, scientific progress, and friendly, social cooperation shouldn't continue far into the future.

The rising adult Adaptives behind them have some serious doubts, which they begin expressing politely but persistently. "Is this all there is?" asked Silent generation women, feeling trapped and stunted in their shiny new suburbs filled with bridge clubs and PTA meetings. "Is this all there is?" asked Enlightener generation minorities, subject to fugitive slave laws, or targets of plans to send them back to Africa for resettlement. "Is this all there is?" asked Progressive generation workers, who saw ambition rewarded only for those of the right race, sex, or ethnic group. As Adaptives prepare to move into midlife and into leadership, they muse over new possibilities and promise themselves that things will be different.

"Damn right things will be different!" say the new Idealists emerging from youth. Where Civics see teamwork, young Idealists see groupthink and loss of individuality. Civics value order, harmony, and prosperity; but the fresh Idealists see these as stifling conformity and soul-deadening materialism. Transcendentalist Ralph Waldo Emerson voiced every Idealist generation's complaint when he denounced the Republican Civics of his day: "The materialist insists on facts, on history, on the force of circumstances, and the animal wants of man; the idealist on the power of Thought and Will, on inspiration, on miracle, in individual culture."[1]

Economy

The economy in a Second Turning runs into difficulties, many of which can be explained by the generational shift from the First Turning. The Civics in charge of monetary policy have a history of falling in love with the sound of the Treasury printing presses. Inflation becomes an issue as Civics tend to finance their grand public projects with newly printed money instead of borrowing the funds through bond issues. Businesses raise prices quickly to offset the fall in value, but are slower to raise wages. Workers begin falling behind, labor grows restive, and strikes break out. These strikes have a new and nastier tone because workers and management so often are of different generations that don't speak one another's language.

Civics keep trying to run things by the book, but the younger Adaptives argue that the book, written for white men, needs to be rewritten for women and minorities. Civic generation executives can't understand Adaptive middle managers' calls for fairness and hiring opportunities for women and minorities. They contend that women should be at home, and minorities in their place. (As Archie and Edith Bunker sang so memorably on the TV series "All in the Family": "And you knew where you were then/ Girls were girls and men were men."[2])

The book, written for cooperative, team-playing workers, needs new chapters for self-assured, individualistic workers. Civic economic leaders are rocked by entry-level Idealist workers who decry the corporate culture, ignore union enlistment drives, and denounce corporate hierarchy as oppressive, and men as sexist. Since the economy usually depends on the willingness of new members of the work force being to take orders and cooperate, the Idealists' approach to labor derails the postwar economic advance. The economy stumbles under the pressure of these intergenerational cross-currents.

The Second Turning of the 1960s saw a steady rise in inflation and consequent erosion of earning power and savings. The next decade featured stagflation, bracketed at the beginning and end by two oil crises and two sharp recessions. In the earlier Second Turning of the 1830s the generational disagreements over the national bank and import tariffs were so severe that they almost caused the secession of South Carolina in 1832. The economic stagnation of a Second Turning signals an end of a cycle's postwar economic boom.

Institutional Leadership

At the beginning of this Turning, leaders of the Civic generation are decisive team players who emphasize cooperation, hierarchy, and tradition. They like leaders who are in charge, believe America at its best is the great melting pot, and usually go along with tradition. Operating from these assumptions, they are ill suited for what erupts in a Second Turning.

Civics are decisive, but fewer members of younger Adaptive and Idealist generations go along with their decisions. Civics become defensive ("Segregation now, segregation forever"—George Wallace, Alabama governor in the '60s), or grow surly and at times try to use their power to force compliance with their policies (We will draft you college grads for Vietnam!) Civics move ahead with projects that no longer make sense in the new climate and look hopelessly out of step. Chrysler refused to build small, gas-miser cars and brought out a new line of 12-miles-per-gallon sedans just as the 1973 oil crisis flared. Throwing in the towel, Civics lament the changes (Archie Bunker: "Everybody pulled his weight . . . Those were the days"[3]) and pass leadership to the arriving Adaptives.

Adaptive generation leaders value spontaneity, process, and flexibility. Finding existing procedures too confining, they rewrite, then expand the process to encourage inclusivity, openness, and appeal procedures for every decision, all the while striving toward a consensus everybody will feel good about. They are willing to wait and see what develops.

Earnest, sincere, yet questioning members of the Adaptive generation raise concerns about the quality of life, health, safety, and relationships across society. The Compromiser Adaptives were the first to advance the idea that Civic-built society itself might be a cause of social problems.[4] In the First Turning social institutions are powerful, broadly heeded, and widely deferred to, functioning as a benevolent Big Brother. If such institutions are founded on the idea of the greatest good for the greatest number, the fact that some people are left out must mean that there is a flaw in the great machine. So society is at fault, and those excluded are not "losers" but actually victims of societal imperfection. Adaptives conclude that this Civic-built society needs modifications.

The arriving Adaptives lead society's institutions toward regulation, more choices, flexibility, and openness. The Progressives created the Food and Drug Administration in 1908 to check the power of meatpackers and to regulate the welter of snake-oil producers that called themselves drug companies. When the Silents began influencing consumer products (and turning their own Ralph Nader loose on the auto industry), repetitive tract houses lost favor to split-levels that seemed fresh at the time. Rectangular street grids in older developments were replaced by curved roads and cul-de-sacs in new developments.

Adaptive leaders open doors and break down barriers between people. "That's the way it is" is not good enough for these earnest generations. Four black members of the Silent generation in Greensboro, North Carolina, changed "the way it is" at Southern lunch counters by daring to sit down and attempt to order a burger and fries. Sensitive to human failings and weaknesses, Adaptives truly struggle to make right what earlier generations did to wrong various groups. Progressives of the 1920s extended citizenship to Native Americans so they could seek redress for offenses in American courts. In 1979 a Silent-dominated Congress awarded the Sioux Nation $105 million for the decades-earlier seizure of the Sioux sacred Black Hills in South Dakota.[5]

Social Currents

Adaptives moving from rising adulthood to midlife and valuing choices and flexibility often make common cause with an Idealist generation moving out of youth into rising adulthood and valuing spiritual experience and individuality. Together these two generations make spiritual issues the defining characteristic of these Turnings.

More strident Idealists in a Second Turning magnify the Adaptives' doubts about Civic-ordered society into critique and denunciation. While the Adaptives strive to modify a good, but flawed, Civic-built society, young adult Idealists conclude that this society isn't benevolent at all and should be dismantled. "In 1892 Charles H. Parkhurst, pastor of the Madison Square Presbyterian Church in New York City, unleashed a blistering attack against the Tammany Hall political machine and police department, which he characterized as 'a lying, perjured, rum-soaked and libidinous lot who were filthifying our entire municipal life, making New York a very hotbed of knavery, debauchery and bestiality.'"[6] Besides denouncing the evils they perceive, Idealists rebel by moving in one of two directions: toward nature, or toward the spirit.

Midlife Civics see nature as a source of materials, something to be tamed or subdued. They see land, water, and their components as resources for the use of the human race. Rising adult Idealists trumpet nature pristine and unspoiled, or at least restored and preserved. They seek communion with nature and admire people (for example, Thoreau) who seem to live a simpler, more natural life.

The other path of rebellion is to pursue spiritual experience. The lofty, masculine God of power and might, and an orthodoxy of rote propositions, leave Idealists cold. They seek a nearer, more feminine God, and spiritual experiences. Whether such experiences are good or what older generations would call "bad" is not as important as the experience itself. So revivals break out and flourish while experiential forms of religion gain ground. The charismatic movement beginning among Roman Catholics in 1967, and among liturgical Protestants in the 1970s, is only the latest example of spiritual questing in a Second Turning.

In each case Idealists focus on spiritual experience, lash out against existing social arrangements, and prefer the natural over what they decry as the artificial. (Theodore Roosevelt, as a nimble Adaptive, harnessed a good deal of this energy promoting conservation and the vigorous outdoor life, and also subjecting the Rockefellers, Morgans, and Vanderbilts and their corporate empires to trust-busting.) Some members of Idealist generations make serious efforts toward women's rights and racial equality, while other members follow different ideals and vehemently denounce such efforts.

Second Turnings feature a variety of new spiritual and religious options. Previously sidelined faith communities attract a stream of both Adaptives looking for choices and Idealists seeking encounters with the divine. In 1968 the Rev. Troy Perry, a Baptist minister, left his youthful faith community and founded the Universal Fellowship of Metropolitan Community Churches, a denomination organized for the gay and lesbian community, but also welcoming their "straight" friends and families. The Hare Krishna and maharishis of the 1960s offered Boomers an alternate understanding of reality.

Even earlier, the Puritans were not the only body of true believers and seekers after God to arrive in America. Religious choices peppered the Atlantic seaboard. The Anglicans arrived in Jamestown, Virginia, in 1607. Lord Baltimore obtained a charter for a new colony, named it Maryland after the mother of Jesus, and sent two boatloads of Roman Catholics to settle the area in 1634. The Dutch brought their Reformed faith with them to Manhattan Island in the 1620s. A colony of Swedish Lutherans settled part of the Delaware Valley in the 1630s. (The Dutch did not take kindly to this last intrusion, and launched a military campaign against the Lutherans, absorbing their settlements under Dutch rule in the 1640s. Their colony ended, but these Swedes left one lasting legacy— their technique of notching logs and laying them together with crisscrossed corners to make log cabins and other log buildings.)

The Idealists in Second Turnings form the mass of new believers and converts that mark the American Great Awakenings. A crowd of 6,000 turned out once in the 1730s to hear the preaching of itinerant Methodist George Whitefield, who astounded even the rather skeptical Benjamin Franklin with the power and eloquence of his sermons. Charles Finney's preaching ignited the Second Great Awakening of the early 19th century. Established congregations and denominations with no history or theology of revivals were swept up in the enthusiasm for extended prayer and preaching against particular sins until suspected sinners repented and converted. German-speaking Lutheran congregations in Pennsylvania, liturgical and traditional, record visiting preachers using the "anxious bench" for suspected sinners.

The generational shift to Adaptives in leadership and the arrival of passionate Idealists at adulthood also cause major changes in parenting, in schools, and in religious bodies.

Parenting

All this sound and fury among adults leaves a new generation of Nomad children adrift to the point of neglect. Adaptive parents do *not* assert parental authority, since for them authority has often meant authoritarian. Having married early, they also explore divorce as a choice in sharply increasing numbers. Idealists tend to delay marriage, allowing time for further spiritual questing. The relative number of single adults soars, and this supposedly free-and-easy lifestyle that does not include children becomes fashionable. (Mostly) Adaptive parents are looking for or creating new options, opening up topics that were once taboo, and in general "letting it all hang out" in reaction to their straitlaced earlier years. Remembering the grim, emotionally repressed adults of their own upbringing, Adaptives go to the opposite pole and initiate an "anything goes" approach to parenting.

Next-elder Idealists grasp these Adaptive-forged options and choices with a vengeance, looking for spiritual experiences and lashing out at assumptions and structures of society. These young Idealists, fresh from escaping a world of workaholism-prone fathers and socially trapped mothers, follow the Adaptives' parenting lead. These young parents are willing to try differing forms of parenting as long as they are "not like my parents." Combined, these forces of freedom, options, and crumbling social institutions unfortunately break down the walls of safety surrounding children.

Schools fall into neglect, and teaching tumbles in status. The new Nomads learn quickly to fend for themselves because adults usually aren't going to do them any favors. In the 1970s television program "Welcome Back, Kotter," Gabe Kaplan played a warm, funny, approachable (Adaptive) teacher in an urban school, assigned to teach the school riffraff, the Sweat Hogs, led by (Nomad) John Travolta. The principal would often stop Mr. Kotter in the hall, point to the class, and grimacing say, "They're not people, Kotter!" School buildings filled with broken equipment and outdated textbooks convey the low opinion adults have of the new generation of children. The Nomads harden themselves against hurt, and work out methods of coping and surviving.

Religion

In a Second Turning, traditional, previously mainline congregations and denominations decline in numbers and influence. Since rational, intellectual Civic leaders typically still lead these bodies, they lose Adaptives who are looking for a friendlier God, and Idealists looking for one they can experience. Many Adaptive parents (the dominant parents in this Turning) express a general approval and tolerance for all faith options for their children, but think it unfair to impose facts about God or religion on children. "I'll let them grow up and make their own decisions," some say. Adaptive generation parents who like options and choices often explore religious choices, bringing along their Nomad children.

The Adaptive religious leaders during Nomads' childhood typically speak of the warm and loving reality of an intimate God. This description sounds out of touch with the harsh realities Nomads encounter daily, increasing their wariness of religion. Preachers who grapple with sin, pain, and suffering get a better hearing among Nomads, but typical religious solutions like forgiveness, healing, and grace seem in short supply. Nomads often find that worship experiences meaningful to adults are not explained to children As in the secular world, Nomad children are left more or less on their own to work out their own religious values.

In a Second Turning, congregations find people on the move, both in and out of their doors. Some of these explorers are Adaptives looking at new choices. Catholics explore Protestantism, Lutherans check out Methodist congregations, evangelicals examine the Eastern Orthodox, and white Episcopalians visit black Baptist churches. In 1893 the Progressives (Adaptives) convened a World Parliament of Religions in Chicago, giving America its first real exposure to Buddhism, Hinduism, and Islam. This Gay '90s Second Turning also saw an incoming tide of Jews from Russia and Eastern Europe who generally chose to remain Orthodox in affiliation rather than joining Reform Judaism.

Younger Idealists go farther afield, searching for intense spiritual experiences that are cathartic. In 1892 enough Greeks had emigrated to New York and Chicago that these Eastern Orthodox believers opened their first churches, giving the questing Missionaries another stop in their spiritual explorations. Turn-of-the-20th-century Missionaries could also visit the mosques Muslim immigrants from Syria and Lebanon opened after 1900.

Apocalyptic ideas mark a Second Turning for two generational reasons. First, fiery young Idealists are sometimes so scathing in their critique of existing society and its institutions that they believe only a fresh start that clears away the status quo will do. So Puritan generation members packed up their Geneva version Bibles (the new King James of 1611 had been hopelessly tainted by its association with that impure monarch and his corrupt clerical allies), and moved to New England to build a pure society and a holy church.

Second, the influx of new religious groups and ideas in a Second Turning provokes a reactionary backlash among leaders of existing bodies. The early 20th century arrival of millions of eastern European Jews, southern European Catholics and Orthodox, and thousands of Levantine Muslims and Korean Buddhists antagonized certain Christian leaders. In addition to publishing *The Fundamentals*, these Christians produced the Schofield Reference Bible in 1907, which in its reference notes and commentary showed how close the end of the world was.

Worship

Congregational worship in a Second Turning expands in variety, either in response to the Adaptives calling for more possibilities, or in response to Idealists calling for purity and experiences. Adaptives gaining influence on worship planning show a strong willingness to borrow forms, ideas, and music from other faith traditions. Orthodox Jews arriving in the early 1900s were amazed and dismayed at how much their Reform cousins had adopted from the surrounding Christian culture. Mainline Lutherans in their 1978 worship book deliberately included both pre-Reformation liturgies from sources dating from the fourth century, and music from beyond their German and Scandinavian roots.

Idealists seeking spiritual experiences and a pure faith led the Puritans to limit their hymn sources to the book of Psalms. Singing in plainsong, they banished organs from their buildings. (Such instruments were too "popish" after all, and were also used by their English church opponents.) On the other hand, Puritans enjoyed congregational dancing as part of their worship, heeding their leaders' admonitions that the dancing be vigorous without becoming overly sensual.[7]

Traditional congregations and religious bodies feel overwhelmed by the outburst. Sometimes they retreat deeper into their own traditions, like hard-line Catholics in the 1960s clinging to the Latin Mass, or old-line Episcopalians demanding loyalty to the 1928 *Book of Common Prayer*. At other times these traditionalists strike out against the new worship forms. Southern fundamentalists of the 1960s condemned rock 'n' roll as the devil's music. Lutheran Church–Missouri Synod conservatives elected one of their own, the Rev. J. A. O. Preus, as president of the denomination in 1969. They then ousted moderates and seminary professors they believed to be doctrinally unsound.

Implications for Religious Bodies

The Civics will be bewildered as the Second Turning arrives. The young people will be passionate, impolite to the point of rude (so unlike the young Adaptives everyone has grown so fond of), demanding, and even condemnatory. Civic religious leaders will be upset by young Idealists calling for spiritual renewal and fervor, and hurt by their children's accusations that Civics are spiritually empty. If Civics answer these critics by defending their traditions and pointing out their good works, the Idealists scorn the traditions as mere formalism and denounce all the congregational religious activity as works-righteousness.

The younger Adaptives will fare better than the Civics in the coming Turning. Their nimbleness will allow them to cope with the spiritual urgency among the coming Idealists, which they may have already noted during their youth ministry. Adaptives' patience and openness to new choices will serve them well in coping with the passions of the young. Their ability with words will help them articulate just what it is they stand for in the religious arena. Taking a stand for something is one thing young, iconoclastic Idealists will actually respect, even if grudgingly or noisily.

As a Second Turning begins and wears on, some of the weaknesses of the Civic leaders dominating congregations become more evident. Their emphasis on a simple and practical faith strikes Adaptives and Idealists as somewhat wooden. The Civic sense of duty can flower into a thicket of rules and regulations that leaves congregational members feeling duty-bound, even guilt-ridden. As a congregational head of staff, a Civic tends to be a bit distant in style. As pastoral counselors Civics are uneasy with a growing demand for emotional depth by Adaptives and for spiritual exploration by Idealists.

The Adaptives' success in enabling and moderating the debates between the Civics and Idealists on either side of them lands them first in positions of mediation, then in pastoral leadership midway through a Second Turning. Pastoral leadership shifts from Civic-style rationality, hierarchy, and a focus on outer-world issues (like property and building) to Adaptive-style warmth, equality, and a focus on human relationship issues.

Adaptives often view themselves as midwives for others, helping others become kinder and more authentic people. With a genuine modesty they will proclaim, "I hope you'll view me as a kind of facilitator, acting as a catalyst for others to ignite their gifts. I believe God has given everyone certain gifts, and I'm here to enable and empower each person to express those gifts and affirm how special they are to God."

Adaptive leaders stress and practice harmony, tolerance, and forgiveness of just about anything except intolerance. They are equipped with an array of therapeutic approaches for counseling. They promote openness, multiculturalism, and inclusiveness within the congregation, and their flexibility in encouraging change alters a congregational climate. They will take some guff from both older Civics, who see Adaptive flexibility as too wishy-washy, and from younger Idealists, who see them trying to be all things to all people. Adaptives can tilt too far toward a people-pleasing leadership style.

Ecumenical relationships take interesting twists under Adaptive leadership. On the one hand, Adaptives' bias toward acceptance and inclusion promotes harmony and mutual toleration, as with the cross-denominational dialogues that opened in the 1960s

On the other hand, Adaptives' love of nuance and finer shades of meaning can catch them in theological hairsplitting. In the early 1900s Norwegian-speaking Lutherans in three separate bodies began exploring the possibility of merger. They handed over the theological task to a panel of seminary professors of the Progressive Generation from their respective schools, who reported back after months of discussion that there was no possible way of overcoming the doctrinal differences among the three bodies. (A grass-roots movement among the pastors of the three groups pulled off the merger anyway a few years later.)[8]

Adaptive religious leaders preach about social justice significantly more often than their Civic predecessors. They view God primarily as love, and that love is expressed through relationships between and among God's children. They shift the religious emphasis of the day from the Civic-style fatherhood of God, to an Adaptive emphasis on our common humanity and our childlike status in the presence of the Holy.

Adaptives earnestly exemplify new patterns of racial equality, but often in a gentle way that can be disarming. They will ride the freedom buses through the South, but they will not overturn white-owned buses and burn them. Like Addie Davis in 1964, the first ordained woman in the Southern Baptist Convention, they are often the lonely pioneers who quietly endure sexism in order to bring breakthroughs for the Idealist women after them.

The Idealists joining the ranks of religious leaders in these Second Turnings give force to social-justice issues. They are often loud in pointing out that structures that oppress are not just misguided but plain wrong, and need to be demolished. Their Adaptive superiors will usually restrain them from anything radical, but the midlife Adaptives appreciate Idealist fervor as a source of energy in bringing about change.

Second Turnings are marked by a society-wide turn from an outer to an inner focus. Such Turnings serve to refresh, reform, and renew people and institutions. This inner renewal reaches certain limits as seemingly all possibilities have been examined. Having sorted through things of the inner world, whether emotions and relationships (Adaptives), or the power and variety of spiritual experiences (Idealists), both these generations now turn their focus outward. This turn also marks the beginning of a Third Turning.

CHAPTER 11

I HAVE SEEN
THE PROMISED LAND

Two decades of exploring of the world of emotions, relationships, and spirituality have resulted in new patterns of life and relationships. These new patterns mark the next turning, a Third Turning, at which time the results and discoveries are turned outward to the rest of the world. Strauss and Howe call this period of testing new approaches and new applications "the Unraveling." Previous norms and social expectations come apart, but their replacements are still being tested and constructed.

THIRD TURNING—AN UNRAVELING

1984-2006(?)
1909-1929
1845-1860
1747-1772
1650-1675

THIRD TURNING GENERATIONAL ALIGNMENT

Stage of Life	Beginning of Turning	End of Turning
Elderhood	Civic →	Adaptive
Midlife	Adaptive →	Idealist
Rising Adulthood	Idealist →	Nomad
Youth	Nomad →	New Civic

<<<<<18 to 25 years>>>>>

In the meantime, in between time, ain't we got fun?[1]

—1920s song

Entering a Third Turning America, society and institutions finally relax a bit from the battles of the Second Turning. People have worked out relationship patterns under the guidance of the Adaptive generation. People have also explored all kinds of religious and spiritual options led by the Idealist generation. It's been intense, inward work, so how about a little fun?

In a Third Turning the economy comes out of its funk, certain social options pioneered in the Second Turning strengthen into new cultural patterns, and technological changes burst across the country. The Adaptive generation's leaders insist on tolerance by all for all. But under this overarching rubric, various clashes between groups, individuals, and generations still flare. The intergenerational clashes often feature moralistic Idealists trying to tell supposedly amoral Nomads how to behave. The Modesty League of Missionary Idealist women in 1912 declared war on tight dresses (worn mostly by younger women of the Nomad Lost generation[2]). The Transcendentalist Idealists of the 1850s imposed prohibition in 13 Northern states to curb the excesses of the Nomad Gildeds.[3] The leading Adaptives mediate these debates and seek to moderate the passions.

Economy

In a Third Turning new industries and companies often begin operating in ways that leave older companies struggling. The generational lineup in a Third Turning uniquely supports start-up enterprises. Midlife Adaptives support new possibilities, and they understand and forgive failure. Often financially stable and wanting to bolster the prospects of their hard-luck Nomad children, Adaptive generations provide them seed money for testing an invention, or venture capital for starting a business. Sometimes this money comes from a corporate source, but often it comes from personal assets.

Rising adult Idealists moving into midlife are creative, and willing to (in the words of several Chrysler ads) to "question everything." This often means a completely new approach to old problems. Idealists begin home-based businesses (using, for example, Elias Howe's 1846 sewing machine), and upstart enterprises (like Henry Ford screwing together an automobile in his stable, which soon became a garage). The Nomads edging into adulthood are often the testers and pioneers, sorting out what works and is practical. Their survival-honed skills make them risk-takers, more so than other generations.

While inventions can happen in any Turning, technological breakthroughs in these Turnings often establish (in retrospect) a prototype for coming Turnings. In the 1750s, Colonial postmaster Benjamin Franklin established a system of post roads with relays of outstanding riders (one of whom was Paul Revere) to carry letters, packets, and emergency messages up and down the seaboard. He also revived an idea from the 1680s of town and colony committees of safety for quick communication and action against Indians, the French, or natural disaster.[4]

Nomads moving into adulthood enter lively markets and run up debt. The Cavalier generation in the mid-1650s used the space behind a Dutch defensive wall in Manhattan for an open-air market. These entrepreneurs gathered at what they called the "wall street" for trade in furs and crops.[5] Virginia planters of the Liberty generation saw principal and interest owed to London banks skyrocket in the 1760s.[6]

The entrepreneurial economy is dizzying, unpredictable, and lively. It also widens the wage gap between management and workers. In 1913 John D. Rockefeller's personal wealth represented over 2 percent of the Gross National Product (about six times larger than Microsoft's Bill Gates's percentage of the present GDP[7]). Meanwhile, Henry Ford's announcement that Ford would pay line workers five dollars a day brought so many thousands to apply that Detroit police had to disperse the crowds with fire hoses.[8]

Institutional Leadership

Third Turnings begin with Adaptives in midlife. The Adaptive leadership traits of creating opportunities, fairness, and tolerance all hold sway deep into a Third Turning. Progressive President Woodrow Wilson appointed Louis Brandeis to the Supreme Court as America's first Jewish justice on the Court. In 1922 Progressives flocked to hear the French prophet of personal power through positive thinking, Emíle Coué. He soon had thousands attending his institutes—and many more thousands repeating his famous mantra: "Every day, in every way, I am getting better and better."[9] Only toward the end of the Turning do the Idealists' characteristics of vision, personal austerity, and high creativity emerge in force.

There are two reasons for this late shift in leadership from Adaptives to Idealists. First, everyone likes the Adaptives. These leaders are easy to be around, encouraging, enabling, forgiving, and great believers in second chances. Adaptive leaders work hard to encourage new people with new ideas to speak, lead, test—and faltering, to try again. Instead of berating a failure with an air of "What a mess you made!" they come forward to ask, "What did we learn so that next time we do better?" Relationships between leaders and followers move from a boot-camp model to a coaching-mentoring approach; or as Strauss and Howe put it, "from macho to maestro."[10] Adaptive leaders seek to establish a tempo and choose the music for the organization or institution. They expect members of the "orchestra" to play their parts to produce harmony and effectiveness.

Second, the coming Idealists are often still busy exploring, and only now, rather later than other generations, they get married, or remarried, in significant numbers. They start having children, become the dominant parenting generation, and concentrate on family, home, and work. Parents increase child protection and become more deliberate child nurturers. They hone their life and work skills first in personal or family settings and only slowly move into leadership in the latter part of a Third Turning.

As Idealists move into middle levels of management, they press corporate leaders to let them independently run a team, project, or division. They look for model leaders who are moralistic and somewhat iconoclastic. Boomers have made a folk hero out of a Silent, Aaron Feurbach of Polartec Industries. When the company's Massachusetts plant burned in December 1995, hundreds of workers feared it would never reopen. Spurning typical corporate thinking, devoutly Jewish Feurbach applied Talmudic principles to the crisis. He announced that everyone would be paid in full and on time out of corporate reserves and insurance monies. He asked for help in cleaning up the debris and getting back into production. Workers cheered, wept with relief, and brought along family members to help with the cleanup. They worked without heat or a roof through a Massachusetts winter putting their livelihood back into production.[11]

Idealist women rise to prominence in a Third Turning, and set new gender boundaries that endure for decades. Transcendental women meeting at Seneca Falls, New York, in 1848 wore bloomers rather than dresses, cut their hair "mannishly" short, and agitated for legal equality and the right to vote. From about 1900 to 1925, the Missionary generation's women moved into three fields in noticeable numbers: nursing (where they overwhelmed the declining number of men), teaching, (as Western and rural "schoolmarms," but in cities and "back East" as well, particularly at the lower grade levels), and office clerical posts (displacing the Bob Cratchits). They worked mostly to support themselves, since their generation had the highest percentage of women to that time who never married.[12]

Thirty years later, after World War II, the Missionary generation's daughters (mostly GI Civics) were being pushed out of the war factories back to housekeeping. Those who did not want to go back, and who were too educated for waiting tables or other pink-collar jobs, found three fields beyond hearth and home now considered women's work: nursing, teaching, and secretarial jobs.

Through the 1980s and the 1990s a majority of law-school students were women. Women form the sometimes strong majority in certain branches of medicine (obstetrics and gynecology, family practice, pediatrics, psychology, and psychiatry[13]). In several mainline denominations women make up a solid majority of seminarians. So in the 2020s and 2030s will law, certain branches of medicine, and ministry all be considered "women's work"? Or will there be a resurgence of men into these areas? Will the entire gender-based distinction disappear? Or will the distinction re-emerge as new fields of work rise in prestige for men: municipal broadband administrator, state director of high-speed rail, or fusion power engineer?

The Nomads entering rising adulthood embrace the options and visionary possibilities that the Adaptives and Idealists put on the table. Eager to survive but doubtful of their prospects in the established economy, they often take their chances on the economic fringe. Tens of thousands of Nomad Gildeds moved to California for the Gold Rush of 1849. A few struck it rich in gold. The innovative Levi Strauss struck it rich using sailcloth canvas to make hard-wearing pants for the miners, dyed a dark blue in the style of Nimes, France—*de Nimes* or denim.

Nomad generations have also faced stiff competition in the economy because of their Adaptive parents' liking for diversity. Adaptive generations have historically opened American doors the widest for immigration. Those coming are typically young adults who look for work in competition with workers already here. The struggle can set off sparks. The 1850 U.S. census counted a population of 23 million. But the years just before and after 1850 saw 2 million Irish arrive, fleeing the potato famine of 1847. This immigrant wave alone equaled over 8 percent of the existing population. The backlash resulted in job postings that warned, "No women, No children, No Irish need apply," and in the rise of a short-lived nativist party—the Know-Nothing Party—whose candidates swept into legislatures and Congress to protect America from danger. (Imagine the social antagonisms that would ignite in our day if the same proportion of our current population, say, 24 million Chinese, arrived in a span of only seven years.)

Parents

The dominant Idealist parents begin raising the walls around the world of their new (Civic) children. As Boomer parents and parents-to-be in the late 1970s and early 1980s looked up to the last of the Silent parents for some guidance (only after inwardly authenticating that guidance, of course) they saw a few things worth emulating (affirmation of worth, advocacy for hugging). They also saw a number of negative traits in the Generation X children whom the Silents had raised: lack of respect between children and parents, with teens calling parents by their first names rather than Mom or Dad. Silent generation cartoonists returned some of this disrespect by producing a series that featured irradiated warrior adolescents who live in sewers: Teenage Mutant Ninja Turtles. Cindi Lauper-style punk hair and body piercing drove former hippies and flower-child Boomers to vow, "Not for *my* kids."

Idealist parents celebrate the newly arriving Civics and join with the younger Nomad parents in keeping these children safe. Idealists do so because to them, their children are special. The Nomads do so because they believe no child should go through what they went through as a kid. In a Third Turning many things happen to make a child's world not just safer, but better than what the Nomad generation endured. Divorce rates decline. The number of out-of-wedlock babies plateaus, then drifts down. Educational toys of great variety appear in quantity. Teamwork (soccer mania), discipline (martial arts mania), and community pride are inculcated in the new generation of Civic children.

This parenting alliance is not without its tensions. The dominant Boomer parents (of mostly older children and teens) are building subdivisions without sidewalks, or tearing out sidewalks in existing suburbs, so that their yards look more natural. Generation X parents tend to keep or build sidewalks so that their children will have a safe place for trikes, bikes, and lemonade stands.

Religion

The religious landscape of a Third Turning resembles the secular terrain. Adaptive leaders expand choices and possibilities for minority groups. In 1759 the Enlighteners of New England watched the first permanent synagogue built. In 1928 the Progressives of the Democratic Party nominated Al Smith—the first Roman Catholic presidential candidate of a major party. Likewise it was the Silent Adaptives who nominated Roman Catholic Geraldine Ferraro in 1984 as the first woman of a major party for vice president.

Idealist generations in a Third Turning split into noisy factions, each convinced of the righteousness of their own small group, and grudgingly tolerating others. The Missionary generation of the 1920s joined various fundamentalist bodies, yet listened carefully as mainline pastor Harry Emerson Fosdick in 1922 blasted these groups in his famous sermon "Shall the Fundamentalists Win?"[14] Some Boomers among the Episcopalians in the 1990s infuriated the hierarchy by arranging for "flying bishops" to nurture congregations and priests who continued to uphold what these dissidents called traditional Christian tenets (for example, salvation through Christ). Other Episcopal Boomers backed the local bishops' efforts to stretch the inclusivity of the Christian faith beyond prior norms. (A recent Episcopal convention seriously debated a bishop's motion that the church reconsider the necessity that Jesus be divine.)

Idealist women make breakthroughs in these Turnings, while Idealist generation men redefine religious masculinity. The Congregationalists ordained Transcendental Antoinette Brown in 1853,[15] while in 1980 the United Methodists chose Marjorie Swank Matthews as their first-ever female bishop.[16] Missionary generation men of the 1910s were recruited through newspaper ads in the sports pages to join a cross-denominational organization, Men and Religion Forward. Under the slogan "More Men for Religion, More Religion for Men," the group held rallies at sports arenas and at Carnegie Hall.[17]

Nomad generations in a Third Turning use business concepts to approach religion, and they consider their next-elders' spirituality cynically.

The decade's [1920s] most popular work on Jesus was *The Man Nobody Knows* (1923) written by advertising executive Bruce Barton, who gives the Man of Nazareth front rank among the world's business organizers. Unbelievable as it may seem, the volume's epigraph was from Luke 2:49 of the boy Jesus as he was found in the temple, 'wist ye not that I must be about my Father's *business*?'"[18] [KJV] Novelist Sinclair Lewis shocked the Missionaries but tickled his Lost peers in 1927. "Lewis (1885–1951) made front-page headlines across the country by standing in a pulpit in Kansas City and giving God 10 minutes to strike him down. When nothing happened, he declared, 'That settles that.'"[19]

Religious education recovers from its Second Turning low point in a Third Turning. Young Civics encounter spiritually active Idealists in their parents' generation. They also find ahead of them Nomad teachers and youth workers who are religiously committed but fun loving.

Worship

Idealists set the tone for worship in a Third Turning. On the one hand, they revitalize traditional worship forms with their passion, and they often rediscover the wisdom and inner depth of ancient forms of worship. Boomers made the early 1990s album *Chant* by a group of Spanish monks a best seller. On the other hand, they often design new forms of worship that eclectically combine worship elements to produce new possibilities of participation and worship. One Minneapolis congregation successfully combines jazz versions of Christian rock, Bach organ pieces, and congregational reactions and feedback to the sermon, all in the same worship service.

Idealist tendencies toward splintering mean that large projects have a high risk of failure. Mainstream Lutherans recently began development of a new worship hymnal to be completed within a span of 10 years. Because of the factionalizing tendency of the Boomers (responsible for the two supplements to the current hymnal published in the past 10 years [*With One Voice* and *This Far By Faith*]), the project leaders face a tall order to produce a successful outcome.

Nomad generations in these Turnings also affect worship. They look for worship and preaching that is realistic, meaning that it has obvious and immediate application in the secular world. They are willing to be surprised, as in the 1920s when Lost generation Pentecostal preacher Aimee Semple McPherson once wowed congregants at her Angelus Temple in Los Angeles with a dramatic sermon titled "Stop! You're Under Arrest!" Appearing on a motorcycle in front of the congregation, McPherson warned her hearers that they were speeding down the wrong avenues of life.[20] Nomads' zest for action makes them often willing to lend a hand to set up and tear down the set, and put away the chairs in the gymnasium that houses the new contemporary worship service.

Implications for Religious Bodies

As religious leadership in a Third Turning shifts away from the Adaptives to the Idealist generation that follows, several issues will surface. Adaptives will continue to press for diversity and inclusivity. They are surprised and dismayed as backlashes among younger Idealists and Nomads develop. The Compromiser generation of Adaptives around 1850 bade America absorb 2 million Irish immigrants and tens of thousands of recent citizens of Mexico, virtually all of whom were Roman Catholic. They were heartbroken that the Presbyterians in 1845 declared Catholic baptism invalid,[21] and that the American Party (the Know-Nothings) could win significant support with an anti-Catholic platform. The Silent generation leaders among the Lutherans and Episcopalians worked out a plan for interchangeability of clergy in the 1990s. They are flummoxed by the Boomer-fired passions both in favor and against their plan.

This shift in leadership comes rather later in the Third Turning than in earlier Turnings. Only now in 2002, as the leading edge of the Boomers nears 60, is the real generational shift going on. (By contrast, recall in a First Turning the leading-edge Civics come to leadership in their early 40s, even late 30s.) The generational shift from Adaptives to Idealists often comes when congregations feel themselves adrift. Congregations under Adaptive leadership feature considerable relational harmony and often display no obvious problems, but a growing number of Idealist leaders begin ironically echoing the early Second Turning lament of the Adaptives themselves, "Is that all there is?" Details, intricacies, and process all matter, of course, but is everything small stuff? Congregations asking for a shift in focus from details to broader horizons signal the generational turnover.

This visionary character of the Idealist type contrasts sharply with the Adaptive generation being displaced. So while Silent generation leaders find thinking outside the box daring and exhilarating, Boomer leaders tend to ask, "What box?" If a congregation's box is labeled with the seven last words of the church, "That's the way we've always done it," it is not uncommon for Boomer leaders to say, "So?" This iconoclastic air often upsets traditionalists of every generational type.

At other times, when an Idealist leader has articulated a vision for a congregation, a denomination, even a religion, others in the organization (including other independent-thinking Idealists) sometimes respond with the *other* seven last words of the church, "We've never done it that way before." An Idealist leader is likely again to say, "So?" Because these leaders are change agents, they are willing to propose and push for change, and endure the controversy, for the sake of what they consider *right*.

The negative side of all this envisioning can be upsetting. In unsettling contrast to the understanding and sympathetic Silents who have gone before them, Boomers can leave hard feelings in their wake, often unknowingly. They are willing to spark controversy and endure conflict in a congregation, but they don't always know how to end it. People who believe the congregation of their faith should be a place of tranquility, harmony, and quiet are apt to be upset.

This leadership transition will not always go smoothly. Unless carefully trained, Idealist leaders show noticeably weaker people skills than the departing generation of Adaptive leaders, and this difference can startle and upset members of a congregation. A congregational situation which, under an Adaptive leader, would have been met with support, understanding, and even forgiveness may now, under an Idealist leader, be met with moralism and perhaps an ice-water question such as "What is the right thing to do here?" The risk of conflict and membership loss rises sharply.

Idealist generation leaders will lift the eyes of their congregations. Vision—broad, paradigm-shifting vision—is a generational hallmark. If a congregation needs revitalization, a new purpose, or a new location, judicatory officials will find Idealist generation leaders often up to providing inspiration.

The difficult side of visionary, principled leadership is implementation. Translating a congregational goal into a series of concrete steps comes hard for Idealist generations. Here is a place where an important intergenerational bond can form. An effective combination is an Idealist generation leader who can work with a Nomad generation partner—whose strength is often action-oriented practicality. The relationship can throw off sparks as the Idealists want to discuss endlessly the moral aspects or intellectual intricacies of a situation, while the Nomads want to move on to possible solutions. But when the combination clicks, the results are dramatic.

Booming Protestant megachurches are often abandoning the traditional senior pastor/associate pastor model for a senior pastor/executive pastor approach. In this model the senior pastor provides vision and goal-setting, working with a small group of five to seven leaders in an executive committee. The senior pastor becomes the resident holy person with a deep prayer life, and his or her major task is preaching. The executive pastor functions as head of staff for daily issues—arranging for pastoral care and hospital calls; hiring, supervising, and firing personnel; and serving as the primary decision maker in the congregational office week in and week out.

When an Idealist generation leader of deep spirituality and a Nomad generation leader with executive gifts fill these two roles, a congregation's ministry can acquire an almost irresistible momentum. If this combination is supplemented by a retired Adaptive as a part-time parish visitor, a pleasing mix of continuity, change, vision, and relational warmth emerges.

This elder Idealist and younger Nomad combination also handles the transition into a Fourth Turning with aplomb. The Idealist leader's visionary preaching and leadership give a moral purpose to the hardships and sacrifices so many are making. The younger Nomads on this team handle the shift to a Fourth Turning crisis as more of what they have faced their whole lives, a new set of challenges and dangers. Those challenges and dangers are the mark of a Fourth Turning, to which we turn now.

CHAPTER 12

HOPE IN THE DARK

There is one more alignment of generations identified by Strauss and Howe, a rather ominous alignment because of its impact on American society. They have written an entire book devoted to the crisis that occurs in a Fourth Turning.

FOURTH TURNING—A CRISIS

2005-2026(?)
1929-1946
1860-1865
1773-1790
1675-1704

FOURTH TURNING GENERATIONAL ALIGNMENT

Stage of Life	Beginning of Turning	End of Turning
Elderhood	Adaptive	Idealist
Midlife	Idealist	Nomad
Rising Adulthood	Nomad	Civic
Youth	Civic	New Adaptive

5 (The Civil War anomaly) to 21 years>>>>>

These are the times that try men's souls.

—Thomas Paine

Strauss and Howe write that once in the lifetime of an individual a crisis comes that lasts for years. They call this trial a Fourth Turning. Some face the trial as children, some as young adults, some in midlife, and some in their final years.[1]

A Fourth Turning marks a social watershed of epic proportions. Scarcely 20 years passed between IBM's introduction of the desktop computer and the end of the 20th century. Yet for most adults 1980 seems like only yesterday. Twenty years also separates 1929 and 1949, but Americans who remember both dates will tell how much life changed in those two decades. Looking at the head of this chapter, readers might soberly consider the regularity of these Turnings and what the next several years might bring.

Economy

Fourth Turnings have been marked by major economic upheavals. They have often begun with an economic thunderclap. The Stamp Act, Sugar Act, colonial boycotts, tax repeals, and tax reinstatements combined to throw the colonial economy into a tailspin in the early 1770s. The panic of 1858 ruined thousands on the brink of the Civil War. When the 1930s opened, the stock market had lost half its value in a matter of months.

Survival concerns mount. Debt loads come due on individuals and businesses, bringing bankruptcies. National and international trade declines. Economic conditions leave thousands, even millions, unemployed. These jobless workers drastically curtail their spending to survive, but in the aggregate this means even fewer sales and less revenue for business. Businesses cut costs further, usually by laying off yet more workers, who spend less, and a vicious downward spiral ensues.

Midlife Idealists are on the spot as economic leaders. Idealist generations in their youth and rising adulthood denounce government and revel in freedom *from* government. (Boomers agreed with Ronald Reagan when he intoned, "Government *is* the problem"[2]). Now as they move from midlife into elderhood, these same Idealist generations find virtue in government activity and in government telling business and institutions what to do. The widespread hard times are seen as a product of economic excesses and speculation from the prior era. The national government steps in to establish (in the case of competing state currencies and state banks in the 1780s) or to regulate (by creating the Securities and Exchange Commission and the FDIC in 1934) the financial industry. The goal is to promote general financial safety for the many. A major redistribution of wealth occurs from the concentrated few to the widely dispersed many (mostly poor), partly from the economic upheaval, and partly from governmental policies specifically designed to promote this reshuffling.

The freewheeling economic policies of the Third Turning just ended are blamed. New economic theories and possibilities are tested and, if found workable, become a successful new norm. In the Revolutionary War Fourth Turning homespun capitalism and land ownership by the *many* replaced British oligopolies and the policy of land ownership for the *few*, while in the Civil War the factory system replaced most home manufacturing.

Government regulation and economic intervention rise. Idealists in public posts accuse business leaders (often fellow Idealists) of bringing on the present disaster and shout down their complaints about governmental activism. Government spending on public works increases, providing jobs for some. Idealist Missionary Herbert Hoover watched construction begin in 1930 on a massive dam outside Las Vegas, which was later named in his honor. Idealist Transcendentalist Jefferson Davis and his Southern generational peers poured thousands of orders and millions of dollars into the Tredegar Iron Works of Richmond for war production.

Nomad generations moving from rising adulthood into midlife, moving into what should be their prime years for earnings, are the hardest hit. Survival becomes their watchword. They buckle down to making do, playing the hand they are dealt, but their situation can become so grim that they rebel. World War I doughboy veterans of the Lost generation camped out in Washington in 1932, demanding that Congress accelerate a veterans' bonus for immediate relief. Instead of receiving a bonus, they were roughly dispersed and sent home by army troops under Brigadier General Douglas MacArthur.

A major depression that began in 1784 was so hard on farmers that they banded together under Nathaniel Shays of Massachusetts with the idea of overthrowing the Massachusetts government. Although the rebellion was put down, the economic drawbacks of competing state currencies and state-to-state import duties exposed the underlying political weaknesses of the Articles of Confederation.[3] Leaders through the 13 states called for a convention to overcome the economic mess and possibly to strengthen national unity. In 1787 George Washington presided over the debates that produced the Constitution.

The new Civic generation coming out of youth into adulthood faces withered prospects and a world falling apart. The Nomads and Idealists ahead of them do not let these special kids down. The Nomad instinct for protecting their juniors kicks into high gear. The Idealists refuse to let their children lose out on the American dream. Government-sponsored programs for youth multiply. Franklin Roosevelt's WPA, CCC, National Youth Administration, Agriculture Adjustment Act, and other alphabet-soup programs were often aimed at sparing the Civic GIs the worst of economic pain.

Businesses reduce product choices to a few standardized ones. This reduction allows for volume production and economies of scale, which lower prices and provide jobs on the factory line. The Civil War Fourth Turning saw the creation of factory-produced, sized clothing for Union troops, replacing hand sewing by tailors with steam- and belt-driven sewing machines. Footwear became sized, and a steam-driven welting machine could put a heavier sole on a new Frye Company boot (founded 1863) than any cobbler could at his bench.

While the Civics work willingly together (valuing the "all together now" ethos of the times), they are not docilely obedient. In 1937 they formed the bulk of the Ford factory workers whose sit-down strike forced Ford to negotiate with the United Auto Workers. Workers endured clubbings from Ford's own hired guards and the Michigan state police but did not back down until they had won.

Institutional Leadership

With the economy broken and a major crisis at hand, visionary Idealists debate who and what is to blame, then set the direction and tone for the Turning. The Awakener peers of Samuel Adams set out a breathtaking national goal: "These colonies of a right ought to be free and independent." Franklin Roosevelt and his Missionary peers looked past thousands of foreclosed mortgages and a 25 percent unemployment rate to rally the country to overcome the Depression and later to defend the world from aggression. Perhaps it takes an Idealist generation leader like FDR to have the courage and vision to proclaim, "Our problems, though many, are, thank God, merely material."[4]

How to *implement* these national goals is the knotty problem the Idealists hand over to the Nomads of their time. In part they do so because the Nomads are coming into midlife, and into leadership. But partly this is because Idealists perceive that these no-nonsense next-juniors may have the right tools to solve a national challenge for survival.

Nomads coming into midlife find their lifetime-honed survival skills and street smarts in sudden fashion. Millions of others now face what this generation has faced their whole lives. Their teeth-clenched determination becomes popular, and institutions look to them as perhaps just the right kind of leaders needed for the times. Through history Nomads like the Liberty generation's Washington and Baron von Steuben, Gildeds like Ulysses S. Grant and Stonewall Jackson, and "Losts" Henry Kaiser and George Patton have taken up the bleak task. It is not by accident that so many Nomads have been soldiers, since Fourth Turnings have historically involved major wars.

Despite their outer hardiness, Nomads have also felt the doubt and despair of these eras. Alcoholics Anonymous was founded in 1935 for the many who turned to alcohol to drown their sorrows and found that alcohol had turned on them. Baron von Steuben faced a seemingly hopeless task of training Washington's raw and clumsy troops at Valley Forge to face the British, the world's best army of the time. On many occasions he would stamp away in exasperation and despair, telling fellow officer Alexander Hamilton, "You curse them now. I can curse them no more."[5]

The Nomads persevere, sustained by the Idealists' cause and by the teamwork and can-do fervor of the rising Civics. Both older generations adore these fresh-faced workers and troops. Transcendentalist Robert E. Lee felt that his men could go anywhere and do anything if properly led.[6] Civics moving into rising adulthood welcome the banding together (a key generational value) of people, society, and causes. They provide energy and dedication to fulfill the directions laid down by Idealists, along trails marked out by Nomads. The Idealists cherish these Civics, and see them as builders of their dreams. Nomads want to spare any younger generations the particular form of hell on earth they went through growing up. Together they invent ways for Civics to help get the country moving again.

More bleakly, minority groups have not fared well in Fourth Turnings. Pressure for unity becomes urgent, and the defenders of diversity and fairness (the aging Adaptives) pass from influence. In 1693 the French-speaking Huguenots of South Carolina were threatened with the loss of their estates at their deaths, partly because Britain and its colonies were at war with France.[7] When a regiment of a Pennsylvania cavalry brigade elected a rabbi as unit chaplain in 1861, it took a year of wrangling and an act of Congress to allow the rabbi to serve.[8]

Parenting

Nomads become the dominant parents during a Fourth Turning. They are adamant that their children should be spared as much pain as humanly possible. Their parenting style is protective against both physical danger and emotional pain. The Liberty generation of Nomad parents in the 1770s took to heart John Locke's book *Some Thoughts concerning Education.* Locke stressed the value of learning, play, and opportunities for children to express their feelings[9]—ideas that sound like a recipe for raising an Adaptive generation.

Adaptive children of the new generation look up to see their parents carefully hiding dark or ugly scenes from them. Lost generation parents took Silent generation children to matinees featuring Shirley Temple and "Spanky and Our Gang." Parents would take turns accompanying their children out to the lobby until the newsreel was finished, then hurry back in for the cartoon and the feature. In 1944 New York Mayor Fiorello LaGuardia (of the Lost generation) read the comics over the radio to these children during a newspaper strike.

Younger Civic parents join in making the world of youth an island of tranquillity and strive to instill the hope that "this too shall pass." The life skills these youth will need will be different from those needed during the crisis. So as the Declaration was signed in 1776, Phi Beta Kappa was established as the first college fraternity to promote the refinement and finishing of well-rounded gentlemen.[10]

Religion

Idealists often believe that hard times bring people into congregations. For them it seems only natural that people having an external crisis will turn inward for comfort and courage. In a Fourth Turning, Idealists waiting for such a boom in congregational attendance have been disappointed. Congregational attendance and membership showed a jump in 1930 at the beginning of the last Fourth Turning, but records show that this change lasted only a few months.[11] Transcendentalist ministers, priests, and rabbis preached to packed pews after the firing on Fort Sumter in 1861. They blessed entire regiments of young Billy Yank and Johnny Reb soldiers in their town squares and train depots. But by the first Christmas of the War, attendance was back to the level of prior years, not counting the men in uniform.

Many congregations face enormous financial pressure in a Fourth Turning. Contributions fall sharply as the unemployed cut spending and pensioners suffer investment losses. Congregations, having taken out loans for building projects in the prior Third Turning, struggle to meet monthly payments. More than a few banks foreclosed on congregational loans in the 1930s. Clergy families see paychecks cut or falling months in arrears. Junior clergy and other congregational staff face reduced hours and job cuts.

One exception to these trends appears in congregations and denominations whose ministry is primarily with the poor. In the Fourth Turning of the 1930s the Salvation Army, various Holiness congregations, and urban missions saw strong and lasting increases in attendance and membership, significantly above the general population trend line. These congregation members and their leaders have little to lose. They also have experience in coping with physical want, emotional torment, and spiritual needs. Many of the newly poor find these religious houses a harbor from the storms in their lives.

Intercongregational cooperation rises. Idealist leaders who stress their unity in things of the spirit now begin to find ways to stress their unity in things material. Up-and-coming Nomad leaders may be fond of their denominational distinctiveness, but they typically suppress this urge out of compassion. Bing Crosby's Father O'Malley in *The Bells of St. Mary's*, who would never turn away a Protestant in need, typifies this functional unity among religions.

Fourth Turnings are marked by a sharp, sustained upsurge in American civil religion. Formal religion and civil religion reinforce each other. In 1675 Massachusetts passed a law requiring that church doors be locked during services because too many people were leaving before the long sermons were over.[12]

In a Fourth Turning both religious leaders and secular leaders take steps to narrow the distinction between religious and political power. In 1684 King James II revoked the Puritans' political charter and appointed Sir Edmund Andros as royal governor. Andros—already royal governor in New York—moved immediately to unite all the northern colonies under his control and to impose a state church. In 1687 Andros seized the Puritans' South Meeting House in Boston and held the first-ever Anglican worship service in Massachusetts. Shorn of political power and finding their religious freedom threatened, the seething citizens kept their tempers until 1689. That spring, the elderly Puritans blessed a rebellion in favor of political rights and religious freedom, and the citizens jailed Andros and his aides.[13]

As keepers of civil religion, political leaders take measures to strengthen this public faith. They encourage symbols of national unity and dedicate civic shrines and temples. In 1931 Congress adopted Francis Scott Key's "The Star-Spangled Banner" as the national anthem. Franklin Roosevelt dedicated Mount Rushmore in 1941, and the Jefferson Memorial in 1943. The Civil War Fourth Turning marked both the appearance of "In God We Trust" on currency, and the proclamation of a national day of Thanksgiving. Julia Ward Howe composed "The Battle Hymn of the Republic" in one thunderstorm-filled night, neatly combining crisis, nation, civil religion, and God in one work.

More negatively, this convergence of religion and state under the understandable pressure for unity has spelled trouble for minority religious groups. In 1776 Thomas Barton (1730–1780, Liberty), a priest of the Church of England in Pennsylvania, wrote,

> Yet my life and property have been threatened upon mere *suspicion* of being unfriendly to what is called the American cause. And with respect to my fellow clergy, what manner of indignities have been heaped upon them! Some of them have been dragged from their horses, assaulted with stones & dirt, ducked in water; obliged to flee for their lives, driven from their habitations & families, laid under arrests & imprisoned![14]

Fourth Turnings have been periods of major American wars (the Revolution, the Civil War, World War II), and religious bodies have faced war issues. Every religious group has had to revisit its positions on war. Not only do conscientious objectors to military service face a grueling personal decision. Their congregations and denominations are also forced to decide how to minister to them. Conversely, congregation members from historically pacifist bodies who join the military do a great deal of soul-searching. Their congregations face a similar quandary in deciding how to treat such members.

Congregations face refugee relief and resettlement issues as families and individuals flee from war-torn areas or relocate to be nearer to relatives and friends. Funerals become agonizingly common, and grief ministry becomes a part of daily life for most religious leaders. These leaders are also called on to perform hasty marriages among the rising adult Civics as the men are called to arms. Clergy and congregations are called upon to support the war brides who become de facto single mothers, and to comfort the young war widows.

Worship

Worship forms revert to classic patterns as worship variety falls out of favor. Whatever is mainline or traditional in a given community gains new strength and numbers. Nomad generation leaders enamored of their newly committed faith and often their newly learned denominational distinctiveness will lead worship in increasingly traditional ways. Cooperation rises outside the congregational walls between communities of faith. But inside those walls, Catholics become more Catholic, Lutherans become more sharply Lutheran, and Jews celebrate their Jewishness with newfound fervor.

The aging Idealists usually endorse these trends. Since it is *their* dreams being forged, they support both the diversity of faith expressions and the overarching cooperation. The Civics in the congregation like order, tradition, and having things settled.

Implications for Religious Bodies

In congregations during a Fourth Turning, principled, stern, and austere Idealist leadership is the order of the day. From the pulpit fiery preaching rings across the pews. The national effort to overcome the economic challenge, or to win the war, or to reach and fulfill this Idealist generation's vision, is blessed in thundering tones. (And sometimes it is condemned in equally thunderous tones. Although one social vision becomes dominant, no one will ever persuade some these self-assured Idealists to go along with everyone else.) The sacrifices many congregational members are making, whether economic ones for war production or the difficulty of sending their children off to fight, are couched in terms of the larger goals the Idealist generation of the Turning has laid down.

Governing bodies in congregations as well as in other institutions shrink in size. Idealist vision and determination combine with Nomad practicality to give direction to congregations. As Strauss and Howe put it, in a Fourth Turning out of the debris of the Unraveling, a new civic ethos arises. "One set of post-Awakening ideals prevails over the others. . . . One Idealist faction ultimately prevails, setting an agenda for decisive collective action."[15]

Emerging Nomad leaders insist on practical solutions, especially in matters of social action and economic relief. Congregations find themselves forced by economic and social challenges to work together. They offer space in their buildings, ideas, and people for common relief efforts; and a division of labor appears among a community's congregations. Rising levels of co-operation in pragmatic issues please rising adult Civics. Congregations acquire a habit of cooperation that sets the stage for the coming First Turning's marks of community. The Civic penchant for cooperation powerfully aids in downplaying these doctrinal distinctions.

Toward the Middle of the 21st Century

Will the World Trade Center bombings turn out to have been the equivalent of 1776? America had a taste of national unity for several weeks. Temples, churches, synagogues, and mosques were packed. American flags flew everywhere. The religion-state distinction narrowed, with live broadcasts of political leaders attending worship at the National Cathedral in Washington. Thousands flocked to St. Paul's Cathedral in London and shook the stones with a stunning rendition of "The Battle Hymn of the Republic."

Or will the attacks of September 11, 2001, be recalled as something like the Dred Scott decision, or the Stamp Act? These events took place a few years earlier than the Crisis itself, but they were omens. In the months after September 11, 2001, religious attendance declined to levels seen before the attacks. American flags were furled, and troop movements in Afghanistan no longer led the evening news. Arguments between security agencies, prosecutors, the Attorney General, and among members of Congress appeared to signal a return to business-as-usual in civic life. It may take a few years' perspective before we know which of these two scenarios is playing out in the generational cycle, whether we are treading into a normal crisis, or one that takes on the dangers of the Civil War crisis.

Either way, the cycle of generations will turn, and we will see another First Turning. Each generation will enter a new stage of life, and their interaction with other generations will show echoes from the past. Religious bodies will preach, teach, discipline, and minister to their people and the larger world from generation to generation. The cycle of generations cannot predict how the next Turning will look, but understanding that the cycle exists gives leaders a valuable tool for coping with all that the years may bring.

A TRINITARIAN POSTSCRIPT

For readers of an orthodox Christian tradition, I offer a few thoughts tying generational ideas to the Trinity.

With four generational types and three persons of the Trinity, a mathematical challenge immediately comes into view. As my fourth-grade teacher would say, "Four into three won't go." I believe the solution lies in the christological understandings that culminated in the Creeds about what we mean when we say Jesus was true God and true man. At various points in the life of Jesus we see demonstrations of both his divine nature and his human nature. Under the divine side theologians usually group Christ's miracles; divine mercy expressed in forgiveness; and the doctrines of the incarnation, atonement, redemptive suffering, and resurrection. Under the human side theologians usually group instances of Jesus' humility, weakness, human emotion, and compassion, as well as his ethic of social justice for the downtrodden. I propose to use this distinction of the two natures of Christ in solving the issue of "four into three won't go."

I believe members of each of the four generational types begin their understanding of the Christian God from one of four points, embracing the whole Trinity, but starting where they feel most at home. So Civics like to begin with the First Article of the Nicene or Apostles' Creed, the Adaptives with the Second Article and from the "Jesus as human" perspective. Idealists begin from the Third Article, while Nomads swing back to begin with the Second Article, but from the "Jesus as God" perspective.

First Article

> *I believe in God, the Father almighty,*
> *creator of heaven and earth.*
>   —The Apostles' Creed

> *We believe in one God,*
> *the Father, the Almighty, maker of all heaven and earth,*
> *of all there is, seen and unseen..*
>   —The Nicene Creed[1]

A First Article Christianity stresses the creative power of God in the making and sustaining of the universe. In God all things are made and united in the tight bond between Creator and Creation. A person holding a First Article faith would say that inasmuch as the universe expresses and reflects God, by studying the universe we learn several things about God.

The universe is immense, intricately connected, and ordered. Even when we see apparent chaos, further reasoning and investigation reveal rules, or laws of nature. The glory of science is to discover, classify, and describe the links connecting these laws. The universe is full of beauty and invokes in creatures like us feelings of awe, adoration, and humility. That a God of such immensity and power would both create and love beings like us is nearly unfathomable. If we believe we are made in God's image, using the First Article as a launching point, then we will show unity, celebrate order and balance, reason together, rule wisely, and create and build.

It seems to me that Civic generations display these characteristics of a First Article Christianity, particularly when such a generation comes to midlife in a First Turning.

1. *Unity and connectedness in purpose.* Whether building the colonies, establishing a Constitution, or winning a watershed war against fascism, this type of generation likes to do things together.

2. *Celebration of order, balance, and reason.* The rabbis of the Talmud said that whatever is not explained or revealed in Torah God left for us to find out or build on our own. "As God drew a circle on the face of the deep . . . when he marked out the foundations of the earth" (Prov. 8:27, 29), bringing order from chaos, so God delights in our searching creation and finding order and harmony. First Article Christians in particular delight in this searching, and like to create their own order.

In human society I believe Civic generations, with their appreciation of harmony, and their left-brain bias toward science and engineering, live out this approach to the faith. In churches this generational type strongly honors traditions, because these are orderly links to the past. Changes will be understood and explained as extensions of an existing order.

3. *Hierarchy.* A combination of being awed by God and humbled to have a place of honor in God's creation makes Civic generations unusually comfortable with hierarchy. ("You have made them little lower than the angels, and crowned them with glory and honor" [Ps. 8:7]). For them it seems only natural that those in charge should be obeyed. Of the four types, Civic generations have shown the greatest ease with sharply defined gender roles across society at large.

4. *An urge to create.* This generational type more than others likes to build, and the constructions of its members display a sense of order and harmony, whether in buildings, statecraft, or infrastructure.

Such a First Article generation innately understands the concept of the congregation as the body of Christ. Community, unity, duty, loyalty, obedience, and good works (especially building) are all expressions of this particular form of spirituality. The transcendence of God and a sense of awe and majesty are often hallmarks of such a generation's faith. As we are currently in the latter part of a Third Turning, this generational type is in a cyclical eclipse. Its contribution to the church is missed and at times longed for by those who remember its time of leadership. But the cycle still turns; in about 30 years we will see its like again, as today's Millennial generation comes to power and leadership.

Second Article: Jesus' Humanity

I believe in Jesus Christ, his only Son, our Lord,
He was conceived by the power of the Holy Spirit
    and born of the virgin Mary.
He suffered under Pontius Pilate,
    was crucified, died, and was buried.
He descended into hell.
On the third day he rose again.
He ascended into heaven and is seated
    at the right hand of the Father.
He will come again to judge the living and the dead.
                    —The Apostles' Creed

We believe in one Lord, Jesus Christ, the only Son of God,
eternally begotten of the Father,
God from God, Light from Light, true God from true God,
begotten not made, of one Being with the Father.
Through him all things were made.
For us and for our salvation he came down from heaven;
by the power of the Holy Spirit
he became incarnate from the virgin Mary, and was made man.
For our sake he was crucified under Pontius Pilate;
he suffered death and was buried.
On the third day he rose again in accordance with the Scriptures;
he ascended into heaven, and is seated at the right hand
    of the Father.
He will come again in glory to judge the living and the dead,
and his kingdom will have no end.
                                    —The Nicene Creed[2]

A Second Article faith is twofold (especially evident in the Nicene Creed): it affirms the divinity of Jesus and his coequality with the Father (God from God, Light from Light, True God from True God), and it describes in particular those acts of his earthly life that brought about our salvation from sin and death.

Of course, behind the Creeds lie the Gospel accounts of Christ's earthly life, descriptions of what the incarnation of God means. Jesus is born of a woman, calls a carpenter Daddy, and shows some 12-year-old precociousness. He attends weddings (John 2), hangs out with friends, eats, drinks, sleeps, and banters (Luke 5). He welcomes and blesses children; teaches and scolds adults (Matt. 23); shows exasperation and ignorance (Luke 8), frustration, and even anger (Mark 11). He empathizes and weeps (John 11), and is subject to exhaustion, weakness, thirst, and death.

One form of a Second Article approach to God stresses this side of Jesus as a perfected or unfallen human, as a model of what we would wish to be like *relationally* with one another, and with God. Such an approach to the faith emphasizes acceptance, friendship, love, forgiveness, compassion, and understanding of human limitation and frailty, gentleness as strength, and challenge to conventions that inhibit human contact and relationships.

I believe the Adaptive generational type shows this approach to the faith. Adaptives' contribution to the church's intergenerational conversation rings with these relational emphases and personal affirmations. In a Second Turning, as Adaptive leaders come to leadership, and rather long into a Third Turning, they display this particular spirituality.

1. *Acceptance, friendship, and love.* Adaptive generations have a history of annoying, and even alarming, the dominant social groups of every era by their steady willingness to embrace and accept marginalized people. Adaptives have dared America to embrace the unclean of the world and to welcome them under the banner of Progressive Emma Lazarus's poem, emblazoned on the pedestal of the Statue of Liberty:

> Give me your tired, your poor,
> your huddled masses yearning to breathe free.[3]

In our time the Silent generation opened America to significant Asian immigration so that the number of Buddhists in the United States overtook the total membership of the Episcopal Church during the 1990s.

2. *Forgiveness, compassion, and understanding of human limits and frailty.* Adaptive generations have been troubled by past injustices, and have tried to turn these into opportunities for restitution and healing. Sometimes they have acted to compensate victims for former injuries, as when a Silent-dominated Congress in the mid-1980s voted an official apology and $20,000 apiece in compensation to the Japanese-Americans who had been sent to relocation camps during World War II. Sometimes such a generation designs a process to prevent injustices in the first place. Cavalier generation leader William Penn, a Quaker, purchased land for his colony in the 1680s with a scrupulously written treaty with native Americans. Penn and his followers were adamant in enforcing its provisions with a wholehearted honesty.

3. *Challenging and overcoming what divides us.* As Jesus embraced outcast women and Samaritans, and as the early church welcomed Gentiles and incorporated both slave and free among its members, Adaptive generations have strived to incorporate all people into a multicultural tapestry. The Compromisers brought the case of the slave Dred Scott to court, hoping his suit for freedom would open a way to overcome slavery without a war. The Silent generation mandated public-school education for disabled children, and passed the Americans with Disabilities Act to prevent discrimination.

As this generational type goes into eclipse in the Fourth Turning, it will leave a legacy of opportunity and hope that those who have been outside will remember with honor and seek to preserve. The poor, the widowed, and the oppressed have always cherished the intimate and personal spirituality of Adaptive generations.

Third Article

> *I believe in the Holy Spirit,*
> *the holy catholic Church, the communion of saints,*
> *the forgiveness of sins, the resurrection of the body,*
> *and the life everlasting. Amen.*
> —The Apostles' Creed

> *We believe in the Holy Spirit, the Lord, the giver of Life,*
> *who proceeds from the Father and the Son.*
> *With the Father and the Son he is worshiped and glorified.*
> *He has spoken through the prophets.*
> *We believe in one holy catholic and apostolic Church..*
> *We acknowledge one Baptism for the forgiveness of sins.*
> *We look for the resurrection of the dead,*
> *and the life of the world to come. Amen.*
> —The Nicene Creed[4]

Christians who take a Third Article approach to the faith begin their understanding of God from an encounter with the Holy Spirit. Such an approach emphasizes the immediacy of the Spirit in individuals and groups, who sense themselves embraced by a holy joy and love by an immanent God. The experience is elevating and vivid, and makes a lasting impact on an individual's faith.

I believe the Idealist generational type takes such an approach to the faith. This sort of generation produces a high proportion of mystics and martyrs, radicals and reformers. They are attracted by the sacred, seeking after (and in various spiritual exercises and experiences *finding*) the God present with us in Spirit and in power. Starting already in a Second Turning, through a Third Turning when such generations come to leadership, and even rather long into a Fourth Turning, such generations' leaders display this particular perspective.

1. *Individual spiritual experiences.* Such Christians seek and claim manifestations of spiritual gifts given by the Spirit for the building up of the

body of believers. Speaking in tongues, healings, and prophetic utterances are expected, even made into litmus tests of one's spirituality. The Puritans granted full membership only to those who could recount a conversion experience. Evangelical author and teacher Randall Balmer writes of the Awakener generation, "What Pietists of all persuasions held in common was . . . a call for experiential or experimental religion, strongly sexual imagery, and an emphasis on mystical introspection, known in the argot of 18th century Pietism as self-knowledge."[5]

2. *Spiritual wanderlust.* Individuals who have had a close encounter with God often seek to repeat the experience. This thirst often drives them from place to place in their spiritual journeys, a characteristic of Idealist generations in rising adulthood and beyond.

3. *Small groups and human perfectionism.* In their wanderings such seekers often look in other denominations and even other religions for people with like experiences. Finding such others, they often form small groups for prayer, study, retreats, and mutual accountability. Together they seek to live life together as an outer expression of their inner faith. Idealist generations in their rising adulthood have shown such patterns.

This tendency has both a benign and a malignant side. Benignly this impulse lies behind the formation of various sectarian groupings like the Amish. They adopt a distinct way of life, often calling it simple or plain for the sake of keeping focused on things of the spirit. More disturbingly, such small groups of true believers can begin to believe themselves perfect, a conviction that classical theologians have always called sin. They begin to follow thinkers like Transcendentalist revival leader Charles Finney. As professor of theology at Oberlin College, in Ohio, after 1835, Finney told his students that men could grow in grace until they reached a state of virtual sinlessness.[6]

4. *Reform and renewal.* Idealist generations shake and renew the church as great reformers or as martyrs, calling for a spiritually alive inner life. They are radicals in the church in the full Latin sense of the word *radicale*, roots, calling the church back to its origins with a vehement analysis of what has gone wrong, when and where, and also what needs to be jettisoned to return to the true faith. Experience trumps tradition for them, so they are willing to tear down and start anew.

5. *Egalitarian impulses.* Since the Spirit can visit any person, Third Article Christians often see no reason for human divisions, and have commendably tried to live in this spiritual unity. Idealist generations often

carried over this equality in things of the Spirit to ignore race, gender, and class distinctions. Transcendent black Sojourner Truth preached to whites. Men like Awakener John Woolman would not rest until his Quakers embraced full equality of African Americans and made ending slavery an official church position.

The Idealist form of spirituality stresses the immanence of God and is open to the immediate experience of the Spirit. Such generations have sought and found the living God of their hopes.

Second Article: Jesus as God

The Second Article can be seen through two perspectives, Jesus as human and Jesus as God. I noted the human perspective earlier. Theologians characterize approaching the faith from the Jesus-as-God perspective as a high Christology. Such a reading of the faith takes the Incarnation very seriously—that in Jesus, *God* is among us in human form. To bring about our salvation from sin and death, God in Christ is willing to undergo betrayal, arrest, trial, crucifixion, and death. By his resurrection Christ disables death and opens the kingdom of God to redeemed sinners. In other words, a high Christology stems from the events of Holy Week.

This Second Article approach stresses the reality of our fallen condition, the agony of separation from God and the despair of death. It also unflinchingly proclaims that we experience the love of God in Christ's willingness to do for us what we could not do for ourselves: shatter sin and overcome the power of death.

I believe the Nomad type of generation comes closest to this sort of theology in the classic Christian faith. As Nomads come to leadership in a Fourth Turning, they have faced the bleakest prospects and most troubled social conditions of all the generations. They do not flinch but often face the worst the world metes out; they face it for the sake of those they lead.

1. *Realism and endurance.* When Jesus protected the woman caught in adultery from a self-righteous crowd of stone-throwers (John 8), he challenged the accusers with the words: "Let anyone among you who is without sin be the first to throw a stone at her" (v. 7). No one thought of challenging his sinlessness. He then dismissed the woman with the words, "Neither do I condemn you. Go your way, and from now on do not sin again" (v. 11). This form of a Second Article faith understands our sinful

power to hurt and take advantage of one another, and our crying need for God's forgiveness and mercy. Nomad generations have lived through unstable and even dangerous childhoods, and have worked in wildly varying economic climates. They have often been treated with contempt and scorn. British officers in the French and Indian Wars considered colonial militia of Washington's Liberty generation dogs and riffraff, while their next-elder Awakener chaplains "prayed for God's blessing upon the *small* number of saints that appear among us."[7]

Wary and skeptical, Nomad generations are nonetheless willing to be persuaded of God's goodness and mercy. A God willing to share our life, work hard in a carpenter's shop, and talk bluntly to the outwardly religious people pricks the ears of Nomad generations.

2. *Willingness to sacrifice and care for the weak.* For us and for our salvation Christ works the works of God among us. He protects and defends his own, even in the Garden of Gethsemane: "If you are looking for me, let these men go" (John 18:8), says Jesus at his arrest. When Peter wants to make a fight of it, Jesus restrains him from a useless martyrdom. Before Caiaphas, Pilate, and Herod, Jesus endures mockery, injustice, and a flogging, then goes to the cross for a cruel death. Why? "No one has greater love than this, to lay down one's life for one's friends" (John 15:13).

Nomad generations have produced officers and leaders who truly lived by the motto "Nothing is too good for the troops." Stonewall Jackson during the Civil War not only directed his troops to rest 10 minutes every hour but also ordered that they lie down. "A man rests all over when he lies down."[8] The mid-20th century Lost leaders and members imposed marginal tax rates as high as 91 percent so that coming generations would have chances they never had.[9]

3. *An open acceptance of others for the work.* Jesus calls a reluctant Nathaniel and a humbled Peter as his disciples. A scorned tax collector like Matthew is also enrolled. Such a God, who respects the wariness, self-doubts, and second thoughts of nonbelievers on the brink of believing, appeals to Nomad generations.

In Virtual Faith, Generation X writer Tom Beaudoin writes of his own generation, "Life on the margins, on the boundary, demonstrates Xers' willingness to keep their horizons open, to live unfinished lives. In this openness to the future, people can find real religious truth."[10]

4. *Rejoicing.* Jesus eats and drinks with everyone, from the overtly righteous to the simply pious to the known outcasts. While salvation is

serious business, the goal of salvation is joy—joy full and joy unshakable. This joy in the meals of Jesus hints at the feasts to come. Children press forward for a blessing despite the sour objections of religious adults. And of course the resurrection is the ultimate reason for rejoicing, for a meal at Emmaus or for a banquet around the altar.

Nomad generations have a reputation for hearty extravagance. Often this behavior has been a diversion from despair or pain. They eat, drink, and make merry, for too often they have known that tomorrow may bring death. But their instinct for the joy of the moment may have something more behind it. In a memorable episode of "M*A*S*H," the company clerk and animal lover Radar O'Reilly finds a wounded horse. He nurses Sophie back to health with the help of his co-workers. He then gives Sophie as a gift to (Lost generation leader) Colonel Sherman Potter, a former cavalryman. Potter is moved to tears, and Sophie becomes his tenderly cared for pride and joy.

We cannot always be somber or serious, not when our God even gives his Son's life so that we may live in joy. Generation X has not only brought weddings back from the meadows and forest glades into the church again. Xers are willing to spend (or ask their parents to spend) far more on the reception than on the ceremony so that the celebration will be memorable far into the night. After all, how can we fast when the bridegroom is among us?

Of all generational types, perhaps the Nomads have the hardest lives to live. It may also be that because of this hardship they find their faith a true comfort and solid rock while "all other ground is sinking sand." Their spirituality comes off as hearty and joy-filled, coupled with a keen sense of the pain and darkness that each of us faces in many ways in our lives.

Faithful Generations

The generations rise and pass, each leaving a distinct legacy for those who come after them. Each generation worships God and lives out its faith with a distinct spirituality, and the church is renewed because of the turning of the generations. If this book helps leaders be more effective in their ministry among God's people, and if it helps readers better understand their companions along their faith journeys, then I believe the church can better live out its mission in the world.

Preface

1. William Strauss and Neil Howe, *Generations: The History of America's Future from 1584 to 2069* (New York: William Morrow, 1991), 16.

Chapter 1

1. Beverly Cohn, *What a Year it Was! 1958* (Marina del Ray, Calif.: MMS Publishing, 1997), 89.

2. Cohn, *What a Year It Was!*, 89.

Chapter 2

1. Strauss and Howe, *Generations*, 60.

2. Shelby Foote, *The Civil War: Fort Sumter to Perryville* (New York: Random House, 1986), 370.

3. Foote, *Civil War*, Fort Sumter, 524.

4. www.ourredeemerlcms.org/ray0100.htm

Chapter 3

1. Strauss and Howe, *Generations*, 121.

2. Strauss and Howe, *Generations*, 137.

3. Strauss and Howe, *Generations*, 223.

4. Strauss and Howe, *Generations*, 187.

5. George Bedell, Leo Sandon, and Charles Wellborn, *Religion in America*, 2nd ed. (New York: Macmillan, 1982), 232.

6. Earle Cairns, *Christianity in the United States* (Chicago: Moody Press, 1964), 60.

Chapter 4

1. quickfacts.census.gov/qfd/. Select "Florida" from drop-down list.

2. Strauss and Howe, *Generations*, 254, 258-259.

3. Strauss and Howe, *Generations*, 268-269, 274-276.

4. www.businessweek.com/chapter/mirage.htm

5. www.ushistory.org/franklin/declaration/

6. Strauss and Howe, *Generations*, 226.

7. William Strauss and Neil Howe, *The Fourth Turning* (New York: Broadway Books, 1997), 221.

8. Strauss and Howe, *Generations*, 143.

Chapter 5

1. www.urbanlegends.com. A site that collects, debunks, or verifies urban legends. Follow links to "Gum Chewing."

2. William Manchester, *The Glory and the Dream* (Boston: Little, Brown & Co., 1974), 576.

3. Strauss and Howe, *Generations*, 284.

4. Bob Hilliard, lyricist, "Our Day Will Come"; music by Mort Garson. (Toronto: Canadian-American Music, 1963), recorded by Ruby and the Romantics.

5. Malvina Reynolds, "Little Boxes and Other Handmade Songs" (New York: Oak Publications, 1964).

6. www.blacksaganews.com. Follow links to "Gallery/Bio," to "Photo Gallery," to "Allen, Richard."

7. Strauss and Howe, *Generations*, 284.

8. womenshistory.about.com/cs/60s70s/. Follow link to "Feminist Chronicles 1953–1993," to "1970."

9. www.loyno.edu/~wessing/docs/KeyDatesJudaism.html

10. www.ajhs.org/publications/chapters/index.cfm. Follow link to "Chapter 32."

11. Strauss and Howe, *Generations*, 285.

12. Strauss and Howe, *Generations*, 285.

13. Strauss and Howe, *Generations*, 145.

14. www.uua.org/uuhs/duub/articles/hoseaballou.html

15. Strauss and Howe, *Generations*, 292.

16. Alexs Pate, David Franzoni, and Steven Zaillan, *Amistad: A Novel* (New York: Signet, 1997).

Chapter 6

1. Strauss and Howe, *Generations*, 199.

2. Strauss and Howe, *Generations*, 199.

3. www.tracetech.net/santa/29.htm

4. Shelby Foote, *The Civil War: Red River to Appomattox* (New York: Random House, 1986), 1040.

5. Strauss and Howe, *Generations*, 199.

6. John Sherrill, *They Speak with Other Tongues* (New York: McGraw-Hill Book Co., 1961), 36.

7. Daniel Reid, ed., *Concise Dictionary of Christianity in America* (Downers Grove, Ill.: InterVarsity Press, 1998), 39.

8. Caroline Zilboorg, ed. *Women's Firsts* (Detroit: Gale Research, 1997), 369.

9. Reid, *Concise Dictionary*, 39.

10. R. Laurence Moore, *Religious Outsiders and the Making of America* (New York: Oxford University Press, 1986), 78.

11. Reid, *Concise Dictionary*, 39.

12. Randall Balmer, *Blessed Assurance: A History of Evangelicalism in America* (Boston: Beacon Press, 1999), 45.

13. www.oberlin.edu/newserv/facts.html

14. Gorton Carruth, *The Encyclopedia of American Facts and Dates* (New York: HarperCollins, 1993).

15. www.alabaster-jars.com/timeline1800s.html

16. Donald Dayton, "The Holiness and Pentecostal Churches: Emerging from Cultural Isolation," *The Christian Century*, Aug.15–22, 1979: 786.

17. Strauss and Howe, *Generations*, 239.

18. Strauss and Howe, *Generations*, 126.

19. Strauss and Howe, *Generations*, 90.

20. Strauss and Howe, *Generations*, 204.

21. www.constitutioncenter.org/resources/site_contributors/beeman/beeman.asp

Chapter 7

1. Strauss and Howe, *Generations*, 324.

2. Strauss and Howe, *Generations*, 329.

3. Strauss and Howe, *Generations*, 133.

4. Strauss and Howe, *Generations*, 326.

5. Strauss and Howe, *Generations*, 168.

6. Strauss and Howe, *Generations*, 167.

7. Strauss and Howe, *Generations*, 320, 326.

8. www.stopchildlabor.org/USchildlabor/enforcementoverview.htm

9. Strauss and Howe, *Generations*, 251.

10. Strauss and Howe, *Generations*, 133.

11. Strauss and Howe, *The Fourth Turning*, 217.

12. Bruce Lancaster and J. H. Plumb, *The American Heritage Book of the Revolution* (New York: Dell, 1958), 19.

13. Lancaster and Plumb, *Book of the Revolution*, 54.

14. Winery Tour Pamphlet (Put-in-Bay, Ohio: Lonz Winery, n.d.).

15. Strauss and Howe, *Generations*, 409.

16. Strauss and Howe, *The Fourth Turning*, 239.

17. Lancaster and Plumb, *Book of the Revolution*, 356.

18. Sydney Ahlstrom, *A Religious History of the American People* (New Haven, Ct.: Yale University Press, 1972), 743.

19. Carruth, *American Facts and Dates*, 105.

20. www.baberuth.com. Follow link to "Famous Words."

21. Strauss and Howe, *Generations*, 254.

22. Strauss and Howe, *Generations*, 259.

23. Strauss and Howe, *Generations*, 170.

24. Strauss and Howe, *Generations*, 165.

25. Bedell, et al., *Religion in America*, 60.

26. Strauss and Howe, *Generations*, 132, 135, 210.

Chapter 8

1. Strauss and Howe, *Generations*, 270.

2. Strauss and Howe, *Generations*, 92.

3. Strauss and Howe, *The Fourth Turning*, 122.

4. Strauss and Howe, *Generations*, 339.

5. www.pbs.org/wgbh/pages/frontline/shows/fuster/lessons/outcomes.html

6. J. Michael Harris, "Consumers Pay a Premium for Organic Baby Food," USDA publications at www.ers.usda.gov/publications/foodreview/aug1997/may97d.pdf

7. State of Minnesota. "Laws Regulating the Employment of Children (St. Paul: State of Minnesota, 1913), 19.

8. Strauss and Howe, *Generations*, 269.

9. Ann Braude, *Women and American Religion* (New York: Oxford University Press, 2000), 17.

10. Strauss and Howe, *Generations*, 223.

11. Strauss and Howe, *Generations*, 223.

12. www.reagan.utexas.edu/resource/speeches/1984/84oct.htm. Reagan's speeches have been organized by date and occasion.

13. Strauss and Howe, *Generations*, 160.

14. Strauss and Howe, *Generations*, 199.

15. Strauss and Howe, *Generations*, 306.

16. Will Herberg, *Protestant-Catholic-Jew: An Essay in American Religious Sociology* (Garden City, N.Y.: Doubleday, 1960), 47.

17. Ahlstrom, *A Religious History*, 267.

18. Strauss and Howe, *Generations*, 139.

19. Bedell et al., *Religion in America*, 221.

20. Cohn, *What a Year!*, 102, 75.

21. George Barna, *The Index of Leading Spiritual Indicators* (Dallas: Word Publishing, 1996), 84.

Chapter 9

1. Lambort, Louis (pseudonym of Patrick Sarsfield Gilmore), lyricist-composer, "When Johnny Comes Marching Home" (Boston: Henry Tolman & Co., 1863).

2. Shi, David, and George Tindall, *America: A Narrative History* (New York: W.W. Norton & Co., 1998), 1423.

3. Strauss and Howe, *The Fourth Turning*, 146.

4. Strauss and Howe, *Generations*, 92.

5. www.cnn.com/specials/1999/century/episodes/01/currents/

6. Paul Johnson, *Modern Times* (New York: Harper & Row, 1983), 436.

7. Strauss and Howe, *Generations*, 160.

8. Strauss and Howe, *Generations*, 240.

9. Strauss and Howe, *The Fourth Turning*, 156.

10. www.cs.umb.edu/jfklibrary/j091260.htm

Chapter 10

1. Edwin Gaustad, *A Religious History of America* (San Francisco: Harper, 1966), 143.

2. Charles Strouse and Lee Adams, lyricists-composers, "Those Were the Days" (New York: New Tandem Music, 1971).

3. Strouse and Adams, "Those Were the Days."

4. Strauss and Howe, *Generations*, 183.

5. Steve Young, "A Broken Treaty Haunts the Black Hills," *Argus-Leader*, Sioux Falls, S.D., 6 June 2001.

6. Balmer, *Blessed Assurance*, 59.

7. Marilyn Daniels, *The Dance in Christianity* (Ramsey, N.J.: Paulist Press, 1981), 62.

8. E. Clifford Nelson, *The Lutherans in North America* (Philadelphia: Fortress Press, 1975), 371–372.

Chapter 11
1. Gus Kahn and Raymond Egan, lyricists, "Ain't We Got Fun"; music by Richard Whiting (New York: Remick Music Co., 1921).
2. www.nwmc.org.au/history2/today2/july23.htm
3. www.drugtext.org/library/reports/nc/nc2a.htm
4. Strauss and Howe, *Generations*, 141.
5. www.hermes-press.com/wshist1.htm
6. www.virginiaplaces.org/agriculture/tobaccostaple.html
7. Cited at scottwinslow.com/2002/wealthy.asp
8. www.libertyhaven.com/thinkers/markskousen/wagesrise.html
9. Ahlstrom, *A Religious History*, 904.
10. Strauss and Howe, *Fourth Turning*, 214.
11. Thomas Teal, "Not a Fool, Not a Saint," *Fortune*, 11 Nov. 1996.
12. Strauss and Howe, *Generations*, 239.
13. Sarah Stewart Taylor, "Women's Numbers in Professional Schools Still Low." www.imdiversity.com/article_detail.asp?Article_ID=6516
14. Cairns, *Christianity*, 176.
15. Phyllis Read and Bernard L. Witlieb, *The Book of Women's Firsts* (New York: Random House, 1992), 70.
16. Zilboorg, *Women's Firsts*, 372.
17. Gaius Atkins, *Religion in Our Times* (New York: Roundtable Press, 1932), 162–164.
18. Ahlstrom, *Religious History*, 905.
19. Fred Whitehead, ed., *Freethought on the American Frontier* (Buffalo, N.Y.: Prometheus Books, 1992), 127.
20. Braude, *Women*, 116.
21. www.reformedreader.org/history/graves/ptl/chapter02.htm

Chapter 12
1. Strauss and Howe, *Generations*, 90.
2. www.reaganranch.org/best/bestof.htm
3. Carruth, *American Facts and Dates*, 99.
4. www.bartleby.com/124/pres49.html
5. Lancaster and Plumb, *Revolution*, 202.

6. Shelby Foote, *The Civil War: Fredricksburg to Meridian* (New York: Random House, 1986), 435.

7. Carruth, *American Facts and Dates*, 39.

8. Hasia Diner, *Jews in America* (New York: Oxford University Press, 1999), 40.

9. Carruth, *American Facts and Dates*, 37.

10. Carruth, *American Facts and Dates*, 37.

11. Samuel Kincheloe, *Research Memorandum on Religion in the Depression* (Westport, Ct.: Greenwood Press, 1937), 12.

12. Carruth, *American Facts and Dates*, 36–37.

13. Carruth, *American Facts and Dates*, 29.

14. Gaustad, *Religious History*, 97.

15. Strauss and Howe, *Fourth Turning*, 257.

Epilogue

1. Nicene and Apostles' Creeds translated by International Consultation on English Texts; used by permission in the *Lutheran Book of Worship* (Minneapolis: Augsburg Publishing House, 1978), 64–65.

2. Creeds translated by International Consultation on English Texts.

3. Emma Lazarus, *The New Colossus*, cited in Frank Spierling, *Bearer of a Million Dreams* (Ottawa, Ill.: Jamison Books, ASC), 144.

4. Creeds translated by the International Consultation on English texts.

5. Balmer, *Blessed Assurance*, 16.

6. William McLaughlin, ed., *The American Evangelicals, 1800–1900* (New York: Harper Torchbooks, 1968), 11.

7. Strauss and Howe, *Generations*, 164.

8. Foote, *Civil War: Fort Sumter*, 426.

9. Strauss and Howe, *Generations*, 260.

10. Tom Beaudoin, *Virtual Faith, The Irreverent Spiritual Quest of Generation X* (San Francisco: Jossey-Bass, 1998), 133.

Ahlstrom, Sydney. *A Religious History of the American People*. New Haven, Ct.: Yale University Press, 1972.

Askew, Thomas, and Peter Spellman. *The Churches and the American Experience*. Grand Rapids, Mich.: Baker Book House, 1984.

Atkins, Gaius. *Religion in Our Times*. New York: Roundtable Press, 1932.

Backman, Milton. *Christian Churches of America*. New York: Charles Scribner's Sons, 1976.

Balmer, Randall. *Blessed Assurance: A History of Evangelicalism in America*. Boston: Beacon Press, 1999.

Barna, George. *The Index of Leading Spiritual Indicators*. Dallas: Word Publishing, 1996.

Beaudoin, Tom. *Virtual Faith: The Irreverent Spiritual Quest of Generation X*. San Francisco: Jossey-Bass, 1998.

Bedell, George, Leo Sandon, and Charles Wellborn. *Religion in America*, 2nd ed. New York: Macmillan, 1982.

Billingsley, Andrew. *Mighty Like a River*. New York: Oxford University Press, 1999.

Braude, Ann. *Women and American Religion*. New York: Oxford University Press, 2000.

Brunner, Broga, ed. *The Time Almanac, 2001*. Boston: Family Education Co., 2001.

Burns, Khephra, and Susan Taylor, eds. *Confirmation: The Spiritual Wisdom That Has Shaped Our Lives*. New York: Anchor Books, 1997.

Cairns, Earle. *Christianity in the United States*. Chicago: Moody Press, 1964.

Carroll, David. *Spiritual Parenting*. New York: Paragon House, 1990.

Carruth, Gorton. *The Encyclopedia of American Facts and Dates*. New York: HarperCollins, 1993.

Cohn, Beverly. *What a Year it Was! 1958*. Marina del Ray, Calif.: MMS Publishing, 1997.

Collier-Thomas, Bettye. *Daughters of Thunder: Black Women Preachers and Their Sermons, 1850–1979.* San Francisco: Jossey Bass, 1998.

Cragg, Gerald. *The Church and the Age of Reason, 1648–1789.* New York: Penguin Books, 1960.

Daniels, Marilyn. *The Dance in Christianity.* Ramsey, N.J.: Paulist Press, 1981.

Dayton, Donald. "The Holiness and Pentecostal Churches: Emerging from Cultural Isolation," *The Christian Century*, Aug.15–22, 1979: 786

Diner, Hasia. *Jews in America.* New York: Oxford University Press, 1999.

Evans, Sara. *Burn For Liberty*, 2nd ed. New York: Simon & Schuster, 1997.

Foote, Shelby. *The Civil War: Fort Sumter to Perryville.* New York: Random House, 1986.

———. *The Civil War, Fredricksburg to Meridian.* New York: Random House, 1986.

———. *The Civil War: Red River to Appomattox.* New York: Random House, 1986.

Fukuyama, Francis. *The Great Disruption: Human Nature and the Reconstitution of Social Order.* New York: Simon & Schuster, 1999.

Galinsky, Ellen. *Ask the Children.* New York: William Morrow, 1999.

Gaustad, Edwin. *A Religious History of America.* San Francisco: Harper, 1966.

Goldberg, Steven. *Seduced by Science: How American Religion Has Lost Its Way.* New York: New York University Press, 1999.

Graham, Stephen. *Cosmos in the Chaos.* Grand Rapids, Mich.: Eerdmans, 1995

Gunley, Frances. *Protestors for Paradise.* London: BBC Books, 1993.

Handy, Robert. *A History of the Churches of the United States and Canada.* New York: Oxford University Press, 1976.

Handy, Robert, ed. *Religion in the American Experience.* New York: Harper & Row, 1972.

Harris, J. Michael. "Consumers Pay a Premium for Organic Baby Food," USDA publications at *www.ers.usda.gov/publications/foodreview/aug1997/may97d.pdf*

Heller, David. *Talking to Your Children about God.* Toronto: Bantam Books, 1988.

Herberg, Will. *Protestant-Catholic-Jew: An Essay in American Religious Sociology.* Garden City, N.Y.: Doubleday, 1960.

Hilliard, Bob, lyricist. "Our Day Will Come." Music by Mort Garson. Toronto: Canadian American Music, 1963. (Recorded by Ruby and the Romantics.)

www.ajhs.org
www.alabaster-jars.com
www.baberuth.com
www.bartleby.com
www.blacksaganews.com
www.businessweek.com
www.cnn.com
www.constitutioncenter.org
www.cs.umb.edu
www.drugtext.org
www.hermes-press.com
www.libertyhaven.com
www.loyno.edu
www.nwmc.org.au
www.oberlin.edu
www.ourredeemerlcms.org
www.pbs.org
www.quickfacts.census.gov
www.reagan.utexas.edu
www.reaganranch.org
www.reformedreader.org
www.scottwinslow.com
www.stopchildlabor.org
www.tracetech.net
www.urbanlegends.com
www.ushistory.org
www.uua.org
www.virginiaplaces.org
womenshistory.about.com

Hudson, Winthrop. *Religion in America*, 3rd ed. New York: Charles Scribner's Sons, 1981.

James, Kay Coles. *Transforming America from the Inside Out*. Grand Rapids, Mich.: Zondervan, 1995.

Jeffcoat, A.E. *Spirited Americans*. Bainbridge Island, Wash.: Winslow House Books, 1999.

Johnson, Paul. *Modern Times*, New York: Harper & Row, 1983.

Kahn, Gus, and Raymond Egan, lyricists. "Ain't We Got Fun." Richard W. W. Fine, composer. New York: Remick Music, 1921.

Kincheloe, Samuel. *Religion in the Depression*. Westport, Ct.: Greenwood Press, 1937.

Lancaster, Bruce, and J. H. Plumb. *The American Heritage Book of the Revolution*. New York: Dell Publishing, 1958.

Lambert, Louis (pseudonym of Patrick Sarsfield Gilmore), lyricist and composer. "When Johnny Comes Marching Home." Boston: Henry Holman & Co., 1863.

Lippy, Charles, Robert Choquette, and Stafford Poole. *Christianity Comes to the Americas, 1492–1776*. New York: Paragon House, 1992.

Mahedy, William, and Janet Bernardi. *A Generation Alone: Xers Making a Place in the World*. Downers Grove, Ill.: InterVarsity Press, 1994.

Manchester, William. *The Glory and the Dream: A Narrative History of America, 1932–1972*. Boston: Little, Brown & Co., 1974.

McCullough, David. *John Adams*. New York: Simon & Schuster, 2001.

McLaughlin, William, ed. *The American Evangelicals, 1800–1900*. New York: Harper Torchbooks, 1968.

Minnesota, State of. "Laws Regulating the Employment of Children." St. Paul: State of Minnesota, 1913.

Moore, R. Laurence. *Religious Outsiders and the Making of America*. New York: Oxford University Press, 1986.

Nelson, E. Clifford. *The Lutherans in North America*. Philadelphia: Fortress Press, 1975.

Oswald, Roy, and Otto Kroeger. *Personality Type and Religious Leadership*. Bethesda, Md.: Alban Institute, 1988.

Pate, Alexs, David Franzoni, and Steven Zaillan. *Amistad: A Novel*. New York: Signet Publishing, 1997.

Pearson, Norman, ed. *The Complete Novels and Selected Tales of Nathaniel Hawthorne*. New York: Random House, 1937.

Read, Phyllis, and Bernard Witlieb. *The Book of Women's Firsts*. New York: Random House, 1992.

Reid, Daniel, et. al., eds. *Concise Dictionary of Christianity in America*. Downers Grove, Ill.: InterVarsity Press, 1998.

Robie, Joan H. *If I Only Knew . . .What Would Jesus Do?* Lancaster, Pa.: Starburst Publishers, 1998.

Reynolds, Malvina. "Little Boxes and Other Handmade Songs." New York: Oak Publications, 1964.

Sample, Tex. U.S. *Lifestyles and Mainline Churches*. Louisville: John Knox Press, 1990.

Sherrill, John. *They Speak with Other Tongues*. New York: McGraw-Hill, 1964.

Shi, David, and George Tindall. *America: A Narrative History*. New York: McGraw-Hill, 1964.

Spierling, Frank. *Bearer of a Million Dreams*. Ottawa, Ill.: Jamison Books, 1986.

Strauss, William, and Neil Howe. *The Fourth Turning*. New York: Broadway Books, 1997.

———. *Generations: The History of America's Future from 1584 to 2069*. New York: William Morrow, 1991.

———. *Millennials Rising: The Next Great Generation*. New York: Vintage, 2000.

Strouse, Charles, and Lee Adams, lyricists and composers. "Those Were the Days." New York: New Tandem Music, 1971.

Taylor, Sarah Stewart. "Women's Numbers in Professional Schools Still Low." www.imdiversity.com/article_detail.asp?Article_ID=6516

Teal, Thomas. "Not a Fool, Not a Saint." *Fortune*, 11 Nov. 1996.

Whitehead, Fred, ed. *Freethought on the American Frontier*. Buffalo: Prometheus, 1992.

Wilson, Charles, ed. *Religion in the South*. Jackson: University Press of Mississippi, 1985.

Winery Tour Pamphlet, Lonz Winery, Put-in-Bay, Ohio, n.d.

Wright, Tim. *A Community of Joy*. Nashville: Abingdon, 1994.

Wyrtzen, David. *Raising Worldly-Wise but Innocent Kids*. Chicago: Moody Press, 1990.

Young, Steve. "A Broken Treaty Haunts the Black Hills." *Argus-Leader*, Sioux Falls, S.D., 6 June 2001.

Zemke, Ron, Claire Raines, and Bob Filipczak. *Generations at Work*. *New York*: Amacom Books, 2000.

Zilboorg, Caroline, ed. *Women's Firsts*. Detroit: Gale Research, 1997.

Welcome to the work of Alban Institute...
the leading publisher and congregational
resource organization for clergy and laity today.

Your purchase of this book means you have an interest in the kinds of information, research, consulting, networking opportunities and educational seminars that Alban Institute produces and provides. We are a non-denominational, non-profit 25-year-old membership organization dedicated to providing practical and useful support to religious congregations and those who participate in and lead them.

Alban is acknowledged as a pioneer in learning and teaching on *Conflict Management *Faith and Money *Congregational Growth and Change *Leadership Development *Mission and Planning *Clergy Recruitment and Training *Clergy Support, Self-Care and Transition *Spirituality and Faith Development *Congregational Security.

Our membership is comprised of over 8,000 clergy, lay leaders, congregations and institutions who benefit from:
   ❖ 15% discount on hundreds of Alban books
   ❖ $50 per-course tuition discount on education seminars
   ❖ Subscription to *Congregations*, the Alban journal (a $30 value)
   ❖ Access to Alban research and (soon) the "Members-Only" archival section of our web site www.alban.org

For more information on Alban membership or to be added to our catalog mailing list, call 1-800-486-1318, ext.243 or return this form.

Name and Title: _____

Congregation/Organization: _____

Address: _____

City: _____ Tel.: _____

State: _____ Zip: _____ Email: _____

BKIN

The Alban Institute
Attn: Membership Dept.
7315 Wisconsin Avenue
Suite 1250 West
Bethesda, MD 20814-3211

This book is made possible in part by the fees the Alban Institute charges for our products and services. The cost to produce our products and services is greater than the prices we ask. Therefore, we depend on the generous support of foundations, individual, congregational, and institutional members of the Institute, and friends like you, which enables us to continue to develop and make available our resources at less than their full cost.

We invite you to add your support to that of this generous group of friends who believe that the vitality of our religious communities and congregations is of the utmost importance.

To learn more about the Alban Institute and to contribute to our efforts, please visit us online: www.alban.org.

THE
ALBAN
INSTITUTE